Sacred Cor

Sacred Commerce

BUSINESS AS
A PATH
OF AWAKENING

Matthew & Terces Engelhart

Foreword by
Megan Marie Brien

North Atlantic Books
Berkeley, California

Published by
North Atlantic Books
P.O. Box 12327
Berkeley, California 94712

Cover art © Frank Riccio and Julia Stege
Cover and book design © Ayelet Maida, A/M Studios
Photograph, page121, © Mark Tucker
Printed in the United States of America

Sacred Commerce: Business as a Path of Awakening is sponsored by the Society for the Study of Native Arts and Sciences, a nonprofit educational corporation whose goals are to develop an educational and cross-cultural perspective linking various scientific, social, and artistic fields; to nurture a holistic view of arts, sciences, humanities, and healing; and to publish and distribute literature on the relationship of mind, body, and nature.

North Atlantic Books' publications are available through most bookstores. For further information, call 800-733-3000 or visit our website at www. northatlantic books.com.

Library of Congress Cataloging-in-Publication Data
Engelhart, Matthew.
Sacred commerce : business as a path of awakening / Matthew and Terces Engelhart.
    p. cm.
Summary: "Introduces the idea of business as a spiritual community and shows how to create a business culture that makes a long-lasting difference in the world and has people inspired to be at and go to work, regardless of their position"—Provided by publisher.
    ISBN 978-1-55643-729-8
1. Business—Religious aspects—Buddhism. 2. Organizational behavior—Religious aspects—Buddhism. 3. Spiritual life.
4. Consciousness.
I. Engelhart, Terces, 1950- II. Title. HF5388.E54 2008
    294.3'36658—dc22
    2008003631

2 3 4 5 6 7 8 9 UNITED 14 13 12 11 10 09 08

Acknowledgments

We thank you. . . .

So many of you have contributed to this book with your encouragement, your belief in our "big foolish project" called Café Gratitude, your continued loyalty as customers, your participation in our workshops, your partnering with us in business, your preparing and serving of food, your taking on your life in a whole new way, your stepping up into management, your trusting our guidance, your contribution to your families and communities, your healing of yourselves and support of one another, your willingness to share, your courage to create something new, your faith to lean into the discomfort, your strength as an activist, your love openly expressing: you know who you are, so do we. We thank you for that.

It's been said that it takes a village to raise a child, and similarly, when we step forward for any sort of presentation or acknowledgment, a whole community is expressing through us. We are thousands of people strong. Sacred Commerce lives in the hearts of the multiple expressions of the One Being. Here we want to acknowledge all the hearts that have opened up to practicing being one, to sharing, to communing, to workability for the whole, to giving up self-importance for making a difference for all. You are extraordinary and we are grateful.

Love,
Matthew and Terces

Contents

Foreword

My adventures in Sacred Commerce began waiting tables at Café Gratitude three years ago. Work was what I *needed* to do, not what I *wanted* to do. I *had* to work to make money and survive in the world. I walked into the doors of the café at a point in my life where I was sick and tired—literally. I had just been diagnosed with multiple sclerosis, a severe chronic illness, and I saw no light at the end of the tunnel. There wasn't even a tunnel. I'd show up to work, put on my best face, and survive the day. Historically I didn't care about the companies that employed me, or the work that we produced. I came and went as I was scheduled and did "my best." Work was what kept me busy. My biggest fear was that I'd be tirelessly and pointlessly working forever.

Beyond what I was *doing* three years ago, I'd like to mention who I was *being*. I habitually doubted and judged myself, I constantly regretted things I did and said, and I was scared. I foresaw a future of being in and out of hospitals, paying for expensive treatments, and "fighting" illness. I felt stuck. I felt alienated and alone, experiencing arguments, break-ups, and disappointment over and over again. I was caught in my own suffering. That was just the way it was, the way it had to be. *There was no other way.* I felt out of control. Money, health, love, happiness either happened to me or it didn't. It wasn't up to me. I was a victim of circumstance. That is, until I wandered into the world of plenty on 20th Street and Harrison in San Francisco one day....

Café Gratitude swept me off my feet. My training in the art of Sacred Commerce provided the opportunity to transform myself into who I had always wanted to be. Now I get to interact with the world in a way that I feel proud of. Through my participation in this business, I love who I am and the work that I do. I can authentically declare that **I am completely healed.** In these three years I have gained a sense of self and purpose in the world. I have the life of my dreams. I reclaimed my wellness. I am in love. I live a life of meaningful service. I make a difference. I am beautiful. I get to say who I am: *I am the creator of my experience.* And my secret to success is simple: my life reflects what I believe, how I act, and what I say. I am proof that we create our own experience. My proof is in my body, and all over my life. In three years not only have I healed myself, but also I have met people who have healed from all kinds of chronic or fatal diseases. I know people who experience and trust the benevolence of the universe. Miracles are happening all around me.

Not to say that all this happened magically one day, without effort. In the beginning, Sacred Commerce was uncomfortable for me. Frankly, it still is. I judged the affirmations at Café Gratitude, the New Age-speak, the whole bit. I was a typical urban, college-educated twenty-year-old who found "the world of possibility" notion pretty cheesy. Stepping into Café Gratitude was a complete shock to my whole value system. I went through resistance, which resulted in meltdowns, and my bosses, co-workers, customers, and friends watched me go through it all. As time passed, the separation between my work and my life became almost invisible. Every barrier I had put up was cracked open, and I was exposed. I had to face the fear being known, afraid of what people might find. I began to let go of anger and wounds that no longer served me. I grew and blossomed. Being humble enough to be vulnerable opened me up to a new version of me. I've learned to share my fears and challenges, and to discern when I am in judgment of myself or someone else. I can say, "I am creating a story about you, I am judging you, and I am not committed to it!" I can come to the realization that "I am judging myself, and I am giving it up!" I now have tools for shifting my attention and am able to notice the perfection of the awakening, and to praise all that there is to be grateful for. I have the freedom to choose what I want and how I feel. I am no longer stuck in anything. I am human and I can choose to be free.

Sacred Commerce training has completely adjusted my existence in the world: it enhanced my view of money, relationship, community, and myself. I know now that transformation of any kind takes work, and the most fulfilling work is transformational. I *enjoy* being responsible for creating my own experience and believing that anything is possible. Every day I practice giving up another complaint, and taking on a new commitment to gratitude. I practice my affirmations and trust my healing process. I focus on living *in the present,* loving *in the present,* and *being present* in all that I do. Let's imagine what is possible for the world if all work environments could produce these kinds of results for people. It would be a very different world.

The pioneers of the Sacred Commerce movement (and authors of this book) are radical visionaries, and ordinary people. Matthew and Terces are loyal friends, bold entrepreneurs, loving parents, believers, environmentalists, responsible consumers, and qualified leaders. I am blessed to work for them, live with them, and learn from them. They are two of my best friends and the parents of my partner. They are LOVE courageously expressed in the world. They stand for Oneness in every business, family, association, group, and organization. Especially yours. Matthew and Terces are messengers of what the world is ready for: a responsible and bright future for ourselves and those who follow in our footsteps.

I am grateful for this new way of seeing sacred exchange in the commercial world. This philosophy teaches in a most unexpected, effective way: by revealing what we *believe*. With practice, we will all soon be able to view the world as a possibility, and business as a sacred relationship. I am honored to have been working in service to Café Gratitude's vision full-time for more than three years. I have worked as a waitress, hostess, and now as Executive Assistant and Office Manager of the company. *My life is my work.* What better way to spend my time than in service to something wonderful?

To the reader, I thank you. I appreciate you for taking on the project of *being* in businesses. The entire work force, like me, *wants* to live responsibly and enjoy our work. We want to share our money with companies who are making a difference for their employees. We want jobs we can be proud of, and stand for. I know that you are reading this book because you are ready. You are willing to try something bold in business. I thank you for your courage and creative spirit. I know you'll enjoy your adventures in Sacred Commerce as much as I have!

—Megan Marie Brien
Vision Keeper for the Engelharts

Hearing the Call

We first heard the term "Sacred Commerce" from our friend Ayman Sawaf (he and his partner Rowan are the authors of a book of the same title). As entrepreneurs and seekers, we felt two of our passions—business and spirituality—kindled by Sawaf's words. Another of his sayings caught our attention: "merchant priests," referring to a past and present lineage of "financial alchemists" transforming the world through dedication to intentional enterprise, "holy business" (consider the possibility). Ayman's words gave form to a new life-purpose for us: Sacred Commerce has been our navigating star ever since.

With the rise of a merchant class, the Industrial Revolution, and the accumulation of wealth separate from church and state, money and materialism have monopolized the passion of our modern times. We give obeisance in tall corporate towers and worship in mega-malls that dwarf our church spires in height and opulence. Prayer, meditation, and yoga are no longer spiritual paths but "coping mechanisms" for the tributes demanded by the high priests of advertising.

The indigenous tribes of the Amazon basin call us the Termite People. We devour life with a consumptive gnawing while occupied by a world "out there" that leaves us ever hungry. Our consumerism has inflated the ego mechanism, what Buddhists call the "hungry ghost," into some kind of all-or-nothing game-show race to oblivion. The human sacrifice of the ancient empires pales in comparison to the ignorance of turning our oxygen suppliers— our forests—into junk mail advertisements for air fresheners. What kind of culture jams the space on urinal disinfectants with pharmaceutical advertising? Where is this line of worship taking us?

This book takes the view that the empty promise of materialism is now exposed and the game is up, and that the coming exorcism will require Sacred Community. Communion—and by that we mean love before appearances—is the antidote to our spiritual, environmental, and social degradation. For most of us, the pursuit of our livelihood occupies the majority of our attention. Thus *Sacred Commerce* is a manual for building a spiritual community at the workplace. The word "spiritual" may alienate some of you, since a material god requires that we scoff at alternatives and doubt the practicality and sense of those who propose them. When we use the word "spiritual" in this context, we're not advocating the adoption of another belief system, only an authentic willingness to look deeply into our lives and see where we are worshiping something other than the fundamental reality of Oneness.

Business is all about providing a service, product, or experience that the market wants. No business can succeed eluding this point. While ego pulls off the ultimate conjuring act—the subjective separate sense of "I"—we suggest that freedom from its aloneness is our heart's desire. Those in search of this ultimate well-being are a growing segment of modern society, and they are projected to soon constitute a trillion-dollar market identified by the acronym LOHAS (lifestyles of health and sustainability). Our Western culture is just starting to understand that life is an inside job and that our consciousness is the real present. Our success with Café Gratitude entails training a community (our employees) in love as the state of well-being and turning them loose in a retail environment. Human beings, customers, and employees are ready to awaken, and we all can make it our "business." This reality demands that we inquire into what possesses us as communities and as individuals; it asks that we be open to acquisition and occupation by Love. "That's a platitude!" your ego might protest. We suggest, rather, that this is a foundation stone of a heart-based culture, one that is not only necessary to our human survival but all we've ever wanted!

This is a big game. We're all for the cavalry coming to the rescue at the last minute and humankind arising in its finest hour, but the split, the wound, the shadow is hanging on for dear life. We don't think we have much choice. Certainly some will go down kicking and screaming, clinging to their Hummer's empty gas tank rusting beneath their feet. This false god (i.e., the ego easing God out) is persistent. Anyone considering the path of a Sacred Commerce manager, a corporate shaman, has to be ready for some resistance. The obsolete paradigm will give its mightiest tug as its very existence is increasingly threatened. Politicians who continue to deny the fact of global warming demonstrate the depth of the possession.

Our sacred enterprise, Café Gratitude, is sometimes accused of being a "cult" because the perception is that we "make" people be grateful. Apparently the god of materialism, the Hungry Ghost, finds thankfulness threatening. But we are not threatened. It's a joy and a privilege to hold this seat, to invite the sacred to live through us and our Café Gratitude community. We can't imagine better training in developing inner equanimity. Remember, when you take on the chore of being a rouser, you'll want to have space for the rude before the awakening. Sage advice comes from a Rumi poem, "The Guest House":

The dark thought, the shame, the malice
Meet them at the door laughing and invite them in
Be grateful for whoever comes
Because each has been sent as a guide from beyond.

Rise from your seat and greet these "guides"! Being a messenger requires enduring the discomfort of others. Your ego's survival dialogue will seek to convince you that the unconditional love business is not your business. Your Angels of Doing will want to swallow your Seraphs of Being. In the face of adverse appearances, my ego entices me with the promise of escape to Maui and the position of gentleman farmer. Welcome to an unreasonable life. We're the Ones we've been waiting for. This re-evolution is our finest hour. Thank you for hearing the call.

2

About Sacred Commerce

Please don't relate to this book as some version of the truth. We don't take ourselves that seriously. When we regard something as true, then something else is untrue and *voila!*— we have splintered the Oneness. Suddenly there is a tenet to agree or disagree with, something to compare with the past, something to resist, and perhaps a threat to a comfort zone. Sacred Commerce is our created view of business. We invite you to try it on, like a jacket. If you're inspired by how we hold the role of business for a realized humanity, then play with it. If you're not inspired, put the garment back on the rack. There are plenty of other empowering views of business that you can try on. Embracing ours may trigger or enhance your commitment to love's awakening, but that doesn't make it compelling "Truth" in the sense of an authoritative dogma, fiat, edict, or concept intended to command your fidelity.

We use the word "sacred" throughout these pages. For us it is a logos, completely interchangeable with God, Love, Spirit, Buddha nature, etc. The sacred, like love, is a presence, a quality of reality that is always here when we are—when the small, surviving, wounded self gets out of the way. The sacred is mysterious, and while it may not be fully known, it is always with us, inviting our participation. This book is a training in evoking the sacred in the workplace, to call forth the presence of love in the business environment.

What does business have to do with the sacred? What is sacred about making money, being successful, and climbing the ladder of career aspiration? After all, current human culture is like an insatiable snake consuming its tail. Our unfulfilled, overworked, consumer society is destroying our planet. We are in the midst of a destructive dream. Corporate tradition, rampant with greed, hoarding, scarcity paradigms, and blatant disregard for life, is the litmus test that proves we have lost our way. This loss and the subsequent disconnection from reality and the sacred are eliciting the need for a new human being that is sourced by the eternal, a transformed humankind that lives life from inside out. This is a guide for business leaders who can hear the call of the sacred through the dense fog of materialism. Life is an inside job!

> "Start some big foolish project like Noah."
> —RUMI

There is power and freedom in being the fool. When we declare something completely outrageous, we are no longer dominated by the looming shadow of failure and the fear of mockery. When Mahatma Gandhi declared that the British would leave India, his game got so big, the opposition so formidable, his chance of success so slim, that he became free to act beyond anyone's approbation or disapproval; he became a victim of—nothing! As Johann Goethe said, "Boldness has power, magic and genius in it." We know it seems foolish and laughable to announce that business enterprises are destined to become the new ashrams and monasteries. We realize that stockholders are unlikely to warm up to the idea of CEOs as facilitators of sacred transformation. We are liberated by our audacity. We don't fear failure because all failure signifies is that we didn't accomplish what we said we would in the time we said we would. That's it, that's the whole enchilada: no guilt, suffering, pain, or recrimination. Audacity is its own reward. Factor in any other baggage and you add "meaning"— some pathway for our doubting mechanism, the wound, to try to grab our attention and deter us. With "meaning" extracted from failure, we are free to propose that our workplaces signify a renaissance, and that our enterprise is going to birth a new community and a new human being.

If we work 8 hours a day, 5 days a week for 50 weeks a year for 45 years (between the ages of 20 and 65), we will have labored 90,000 hours. With an average 8 hours of sleep a day, this number represents 30–40% of the waking hours of our youth and middle age. Most of us invest our attention—which is all we really have—more on our jobs than anything else. Our employment often requires more of our "worship power" than that which we hold most sacred: family, health, God, and community service. As a result, we end up being martyrs on the job; work is more sacrifice than sacred.

We long to return to a simpler semblance of human being. With Sacred Commerce we aspire to heal this wounded longing, this split between career and survival, between "making a living" and creating a self-realized, fulfilled, and vital life. This guidebook integrates that self-creation, which we choose to deem sacred, with a thriving, prosperous business—a business that becomes a sacred container for the transformation of the participants, expressed as prosperity and abundance.

> "We hold these truths to be self-evident:
> that all men were created equal and were endowed
> by their Creator with certain inalienable rights
> and that among these are Life, Liberty
> and the pursuit of Happiness."
> —THOMAS JEFFERSON

The new American Republic was revolutionary because it was founded on an association of our sacred birth rights—life and liberty—with the pursuit of happiness, rather than on suffering and victimhood. This vehicle for this "pursuit" was business. From the beginning Americans saw business as a means for becoming happy while enlarging everyone's life and liberty, and even though this was often not implemented as broadly or as perfectly as we might like, to the degree to which it became America's signature aspiration it made our New World into a beacon for all who had a similar dream. Eventually, however, the "robber baron" paradigm eclipsed the Jeffersonian ideal, and pathways to business success began to emulate the Old World model: predation and exploitation as the route to riches for the business owner; and strikes, mob action, envy, and resentment became the "class war" reaction of the worker.

A spiritual world separate from a material world is the ancient tale in which we swim. In this tale our concern for survival, comfort, and health are often separate from our relationship to our Source and the mystery of who we really are. As a result, we put our attention on survival—on "feeding the hungry ghost"—while sacrificing indefinitely our aspiration to delve into the experience of spiritual fulfillment. In contemporary culture our relationship with the sacred, if we have one, is mostly a private affair or is practiced in communities separate from work communities. Perhaps because of our smorgasbord of spiritual and religious choices and our sensitivity to being offensive, our workplaces are mostly devoid of an intentional commitment to awaken humankind.

How could a work community even agree to choose what exactly there is to awaken to? How would one start? In the case of the Mirembe Kawomera coffee co-op in Uganda, a quality of the sacred was chosen as a business practice. Here Jewish, Muslim, and Christian coffee growers chose to awaken and collectively work together in peace and cooperation. Five hundred and fifty-eight families have put universal qualities of being, attributes of spirit, and a belief in Oneness before dogma. No one has had to renounce their individual creeds. Peace and cooperation are qualities of everyone's God and everyone's being. The story of their communion-inspired customer support created an international market for their coffee. If they had not stepped out of a habitual, tradition-based separation paradigm, the market for their coffee would not have materialized. A shift in being, a step toward Oneness, impacted their bottom line and led to their success. That is Sacred Commerce! The universe conspires in our success through channels that the old story would have us believe lead mainly to an ascetic's cave and a life of denial. Our attention is on the attraction that is exerted between the awakening of unity and the growth of love in and among human beings in a business, and the prosperity of that business.

What we'd like you to consider is that the awakening is already here and is always happening, including at your place of business, perhaps unconsciously most of the time. The universe is always prodding us to drop the appearance of separation. Look at where you personally are suffering, and you will perhaps discover what it is that you are resisting. The point at which you are suffering is often the point where life is asking you to let go of something that no longer serves you and Oneness (if it ever did). Look at your business. Any discomfort or angst you find is usually an indication of that which no longer serves the enterprise. Discomfort is the flip side of awakening. Thank God for the environmental crisis, without which we would lack any planetary consciousness, any sense of One World.

When we get attached to members of our café staff or begin to treat members of our management team as if they were irreplaceable, it becomes easy to accommodate the wants and desires of a single personality at the expense of the entire business. Then we as owners begin to feel resentful and trapped. Actually, this "trap" is only our avoidance of an emotionally charged conversation, or the training of a better-suited person. Life is already sacred. Spirit is always awakening to itself. Sacred Commerce is the practice of consciously and intentionally cultivating the self-realization already in process.

> "Love is reducing the universe to one being."
> —VICTOR HUGO

Consider that we are born into a condition of "not enough." Not enough love, money, beauty, appreciation, time. To be human is to be "not enough." Give attention to the possibility that all human communication, every word uttered in the human experience, is either a call for love—"Appreciate me, acknowledge me, validate me, approve of me, take care of me, hold me!"—or an expression of love—"Thank you, I am great, you are extraordinary, I want your life to be successful." All our acts and words are attempts to presence (be and present) love. Consider that love, or the desire for love, is the distillation of all spoken words and the motivation of all action. We are longing for love, crying out to connect, we yearn to belong, and we're just not authentic about it. The cost of this pretense is resignation and a cynicism that deadens our lives, our labor, and our communities.

"Take away love and our Earth is a tomb."
—ROBERT BROWNING

Most Department of Motor Vehicle (DMV) offices are noteworthy examples of numb work spaces. The employees feel underappreciated by both the customers and the state bureaucracy. The
customers feel dominated by the regulations. Everyone is just surviving the experience. No one intentionally says, "Let's go to the
DMV and be numb." It's just that we don't feel safe or empowered to connect, to be love, under the circumstances. As part of
our pre-Café Gratitude experiment, we went to a DMV office in
San Francisco and started asking clerks and customers what they
were grateful for. We started directing attention to gratitude, the
universal quality of God and Love, and we were facilitating its
expression. In moments the space became palpably more buoyant.
One clerk reported that she had never been asked that question
before and was thrilled to share with us about her family. Another
said, "Imagine if we asked each other that question every day—
this place would be rockin'!" People started laughing, asking each
other what they were grateful for. Within minutes those who were
participating were connecting, dwelling on commonality, getting
present to what was dear to them.

Consider that unconditional love is the only reality, and everything else is our resistance to it. Notice that when people are depart-
ing this life, leaving their bodies, their attention is not on the
third-quarter profits for that fiscal year. We cherish the scene in
Charles Dickens' *A Christmas Carol,* when Ebeneezer Scrooge
attempts to enlist his late partner Jacob Marley's ghost in the concept of how responsible they had been in business. The ghost of
Marley blasts Scrooge with his chain-rattling shriek from the other
side of the beyond: "Mankind was our business!" he declares.

This little handbook is a training in how to a have a business community intentionally serve the awakening of humankind, particularly the awakening of its employees and customers, all while maintaining the new bottom line.

We all want to take care of each other, but we're afraid to do so. What inhibits the global family is the paralyzing fear of rejection, fear that our generosity won't be reciprocated, so we "save face" (as they say in the East) and protect our sense of our own "dignity." Here is where leadership comes to the fore. Leadership denotes going first and being willing to share with blind faith. The paradox is that there is nothing to protect. In fact, whatever we protect we ultimately lose, because in calling something ours we create separation. What we can't give away possesses us. What we ultimately want can't be lost. Love is the bottom line.

Love for a business as an entity is profit. As business owners we are always looking out for the tender entity known as Café Gratitude. If we nurture her, she'll give livelihood to hundreds and sustenance to thousands. Love of transformation is awakening. Are employees inspired by their lives? Is your business bringing forth a new consciousness? Is your business a nurturing presence to all earthly life? Profit and success demand it. Love of the Earth is sustainability. Love of community is the highest customer service. Are you using your privileged position of entrepreneur to liberate those less fortunate, while cultivating love in action?

- ♦ P: profit=love of enterprise
- ♦ A: awakening=love of transformation
- ♦ S: sustainability=love of Earth or the whole
- ♦ S: service=love of community

Does your business get a PASS? Does it fulfill love at these four levels? In these pages we will mostly be training businesses to manage the transformation, the awakening of their employees, patrons, vendors, and owners. We intend to demonstrate how this transformation will enhance profit and sustainability and lead to community service.

3

Our Four Insights

We have discovered spiritual insights that source and support our business. These constitute an important foundation that guides our growth and choices.

- Create a sacred place.
- Be the space for all of it.
- Be in the game.
- Be an invitation.

I recall a time on our organic farm in Maui when Matthew and I were first entertaining the idea of opening a raw foods-vegan restaurant. When we considered what lay ahead if we chose to proceed, we tried to envision all the potential challenges, struggles, and inconvenience attendant to such a commitment. Similar experiences have enveloped us each time the prospect of opening another Café Gratitude has presented itself. Yet when we take that same prospect and view it through the first of our four insights—*create a sacred place*—we light up, become inspired, and easily move forward into the creation of whatever is next. Consider that the energy that goes into creating a sacred place is quite different from simply setting up a business, an office, or a branch. You are being challenged to bring the sacred into all aspects of your creation, into each choice, each purchase, and each element of design. You are participating in a holy act. You are connecting with the divine while creating a place for others to step into. Can you see that creating a sacred place is very distinct from what you might consider to be the process of setting up to go into business?

All of our cafés represent a one-of-a-kind milieu and resonance. We work on every aspect of the design, operation, staff, and community atmosphere to foster this alchemy. We want people to step inside and enjoy being present to something distinctive, something once-in-a-lifetime that is creating an unexpected experience. We are rigorous about keeping this spontaneity in the forefront of our cafés so that most of our attention is focused on inspiring ourselves, our managers, and employees, challenging every human being engaged in our enterprise to be bigger and bolder in their expression of the sacred, their realizations of love. This also means keeping the space that is Café Gratitude impeccable, and caring for it as you would a temple or a shrine.

When a patron enters this space and begins complaining about what we do or don't offer, or an employee is resisting handling a difficult customer, we remember that *being the space for all of it* is our second guiding insight. This means holding the space for anything and everything, all expressions of life and human being. Some establishments display signs that state, "We reserve the right to refuse service to anyone." We on the other hand say that although you may not be seated and dine with us, our interaction with you will come from being of service to the whole, to the one being, tending to the collective wounds and opportunities to heal. We will treat you with respect and love and interact with you in a way that leaves you cared for and heard. We are in service to everyone who enters our field of vision. This is manifested in our belief that whatever transpires in Café Gratitude is going to be a blessing. This faith is reflected in our creation of "a space for all of it," where being in relationship with the difficult patron is just as much a blessing as being with the courteous and friendly ones. That's part of what makes our restaurants sacred: nothing unholy can happen there.

> *"Labora est ora."*
> [Let work be your prayer.]
> —ST. BENEDICT

We ask that our employees be present to each patron without distraction. We term this "being clear." We also ask them the question of the day. Some days our employees may not come in willing to be cleared, may not want to ask the question of the day. Managers may not feel like they have the time to check in on what breakthrough an employee may be open to at this time. Work manifests in many forms, but let's discuss two of those models. Early Christianity practiced *"Labora est ora."* In other words, prayer does not necessarily consist only of a special time set aside and away from distractions, but in the realization that every moment is sacred, and every act of labor we perform is meaningful when done with a clear mind and intent, focused wholly on the task at hand and consecrated to the beautiful mystery of the moment.

The traditional model of wage-employment is one in which alienated employees force themselves to suppress their beckoning stream of personal anxieties, obsessions, and desires long enough to do the work for which they are receiving a wage. This often leads to customers receiving service that is not really service, but rather acquiescence to the necessity of the worker to earn a wage by minimally fulfilling the needs of the customer. The customer almost always senses this perfunctory level of interaction, which lowers the level for everyone, giving the customer the devastating impression that they are not really cared for; rather they are on the receiving end of a kind of prostitution.

Our insight into the worker-customer relationship says *be in the game.* How can we be encouraging customers to create and play a game of shifting their attention, utilizing their worship power to connect with qualities of the divine, if we aren't? Being in the game ourselves is essential to inviting others to play. Many people have commented on how Café Gratitude employees are actually happy, not pretending to be; how they are present to the customer, giving that person all of their attention and commitment in that moment. These unique elements are a big contributing factor in the success of our enterprise, and this is something every business person can understand: when our service is exemplary it is because our employees are present and in the game! The integrity of your business depends on your employees being in the game; it is also the foundation for employees being inspired in all areas of their life from their participation at work. When you are in the game you are practicing this view of life, and the more you practice it the more freedom you will experience from old patterns and views that have previously inhibited you or your life.

One of our managers had a school loan that every month left her feeling angry, financially inhibited, resentful, and hopeless. We worked with her in taking on the truth of how abundant her life already is, how much she has to be grateful for, and how she could still have the same loan due every month and yet be enjoying the life she is living right now. That is her experience now, after taking on the practice of seeing her loan and her life in a new way. She has created a home she loves, drives a car she is proud of, is in love with her partner, does work she honors, and creates opportunities she couldn't even have imagined in those early days of feeling stuck by her situation. Being in the game opens us to possibilities that are hidden from view when all we can see are the limitations of our circumstances. This consciousness that we offer to our employees is returned to us and to our customers in a mutual exchange of helpfulness and loving kindness that is not a commodity but a living affirmation of how the universe works. Any other behavior is unprofitable.

It isn't always easy to be coming from one perspective while working with or serving people coming from another perspective. This is what the fourth of our insights addresses when we say, *"Be an invitation."* It is paramount that we don't start making others wrong or feeling that our view of life or business is the "right view," implying that any other view is the wrong one. People can only resist, defend, or protect whatever their view may be if we start from a premise in opposition. Being an invitation is just that, a request to participate, come forward, open up to the possibility of an exchange of affirmations, by offering a welcoming and encouraging gesture that signifies "We want to deal with the real you." It has to be okay if they choose not to; we don't diminish our loving or serving them, and we continue to participate with them in an inviting manner. We try to teach our managers and employees to see that a "no" doesn't mean anything other than "not right now." Any other meaning is extraneous baggage. Without that additional baggage we can continue to become increasingly powerful in being inviting and making requests.

Take a moment now and look at your business model. What do you see that these spiritual insights might provide for you and your company?

CREATE A SACRED PLACE

Following are our guidelines for creating a sacred place. When customers or anyone walks in, what they see elicits the sacred, inviting them to think about themselves and others in a new way,

inspiring them, supporting them in shifting from their habitual ways of thinking and acting, prompting them to step inside a
unique experience, surprising them, encouraging them to discover
and take in more, and inviting them to ask questions and open up,
evoking an awakening. There are many means by which this can
be accomplished: through artwork, the display of inspirational quo-
tations and aphorisms, the décor, and perhaps most importantly,
how your people interact with your customer. How do your employees greet your patrons or clients? What is their context for work?
Why do they work with you? What are they providing the customer, and what are you providing for them?

So much of sacred commerce takes place in the unseen, the
unsaid. It's what we call "being." We have all probably heard the
saying, "Who you are being is so loud I can hardly hear what you
are saying." What really creates any place as sacred is fueled by the
being, being love, connected. It's best to always be looking through
the eyes of the customer as we commit to keeping the sacred in
place, and remember, we're able to manifest what represents the
sacred by being present.

BE THE SPACE FOR ALL OF IT

So much of what prepares us to be here now for whatever may
present itself relies on how we see ourselves and how we see what
we provide for others. Are we judging ourselves and thus judging
others? Do we have room for our own human experience and therefore room for the experience of everyone else? We have learned
that a person's ability to have room for all the many expressions of
life relies on the person being secure and centered in her- or himself. Being and staying clear is essential to being able to hold space
for others.

I remember when we opened our first café, in the Mission District of San Francisco, and customers who owned businesses of their own saw us spending time sitting down with each employee to connect and clear them. These business owners grinned or outwardly expressed skepticism at the likelihood that we would be able to maintain this practice. We shared with them our belief that this practice is the foundation for our ability to provide the experience we are committed to offering all our guests. When you have room for your employees and their concerns without needing to change or fix them, they in turn will be able to have room for your customers and whatever challenges they might present. Remember that this does not have to take a lot of time; people can share without telling the whole story. This practice is about acknowledging what is occupying their thoughts, not recreating the entire experience from their perspective.

We consider the clearing practice that touches every manager and employee every day to be the most valuable of all our practices and the best use of our time and money, as well as a great investment in the quality of our employees' lives and the quality of service provided to our customers. (Clearing is a process by which you can simply distinguish anything that might be in the way of your being present. See Chapter 4 for more details.) Imagine being able to relate to whatever challenges you might face with your customers and clients without ever considering them to be "wrong"! This experience in itself is completely transformational and at the core of our model of sacred commerce.

Three police officers entered our café one day and stood just inside the doorway observing our busy operation. After a few moments they moved to the counter and asked us, "What's going on here?" They shared with us their sense that something different was happening at our restaurant and weren't quite sure what it was. We spoke with them for a while about ordering smoothies and coffee drinks according to the affirmative names for these items on our menu, instead of just ordering coffee. "I'll have an 'I Am Courageous,'" said one, while the other two asked for an "I Am Lusciously Awake" and an "I Am Blessed." One of them added, "We sure are!" having taken the time to see how blessed he was. They smiled at the unique experience of what in other venues and circumstances would have been a humdrum aspect of business as usual.

BE IN THE GAME

The game of Sacred Commerce is one of creating business as an opportunity to awaken. This signifies that every manager, employee, and customer or client is creating whatever presents itself as an opportunity to grow, expand, and awaken. There are no bad experiences in this context. There is simply what happens, and then what we create as a result of it. When we look at the world and its people we often create some story, some experience of what is happening that's fabricated in our mind, usually with few facts or little relationship to what is actually being presented to us. We see something and then interpret it based on our past experience or habits, our version of life.

Recently a good friend and minister of our church shared the insight that since we are all making up stories or interpreting the stories of others all the time, why not make up something that opens our hearts? She told us a story of a man on the train with his two children. The children were talking loudly and getting up and down from their seats frequently. The other passengers were disturbed and began to frown at them. Finally a woman got the man's attention (he seemed distracted) and asked if he would quiet his children. The man quickly apologized as he looked around, as if being present for the first time, and said, "We just came from the hospital where my wife passed away, and I have been thinking about how to tell them about their mother."

Culturally we have imposed stories that separate us from others or from a grand and beautiful experience of life. Why not begin to create stories that connect us to others and craft a full and meaningful life? By such a process we can be more in the game. Who would you like to be? Where could you be putting your attention?

At Café Gratitude an eleven-year-old girl was playing the Abounding River game with her parents. Matthew walked over to offer her assistance to enhance her play. The game card the girl had selected read, "With whom are you stingy?" Matthew coached her to be certain she understood, but before he could finish, she said, "Sometimes when my Mom wakes me up in the morning and wants to snuggle with me, I push her away and I'm stingy with her. I could be more loving." Matthew observed tears welling in her mother's eyes. Because the girl was really being in the game, she made an enormous difference for her mom.

BE AN INVITATION

We are always encouraging others to participate with us in all sorts of activities such as sharing dinner, seeing movies, donating money, taking a trip, signing up for a seminar or a class. We know when our requests are heard as an invitation because people say yes, they want to join in and play with us. That doesn't mean they don't have things to work out, like the finances, scheduling, baby-sitting, etc. It does mean that they work to see how they can make it happen, not whether or not it will happen. If they decline our invitation we respond as though there were nothing wrong, because (simply stated) there isn't. They just can't make it happen at the time. However, if your requests are not being presented as an opportunity for others, you probably are not truly inviting them. You may have only a lukewarm desire for them to join you, feel indifferent about it, or simply be coming from some position that makes them feel like they're obligated to join you. Imagine if each request made of you were a true invitation, how full and rich would your experience of life be? When you are a "yes" to life, life is a "yes" to you.

Recently I invited my children to make a trip to Oregon with us to celebrate their birth father's sixtieth birthday. He is a Vietnam vet who didn't come back in great shape, and we had divorced more than twenty-five years ago. He has three grandchildren he had never met. I really wanted them to come, but I also knew it was important for me to be okay if they chose not to. They did choose to make the trip, and it was so healing for all of us. I am grateful that my request occurred as an invitation to them.

4

Clear on Clearing

"In the carriages of the past
you can't go anywhere."
—MAXIM GORKY

C learing is the foundation of Sacred Commerce. The clearing is an access to the present moment, the only known location of the sacred. The degree to which we dwell on the past is the degree to which we limit our transformation. Clearing is a basic technique for distinguishing how the past is impacting the present and then presenting an opportunity to create something new and shift one's attention to something more empowering. At Café Gratitude, our district manager starts clearing the general managers at 7:45 a.m. They in turn clear the managers, who then begin the clearing of our front-line employees, one on one and in groups as they start their shifts. At Café Gratitude we clear about 110 people a day, 360 days a year. We figure the expense of this endeavor is about $230,000 per year (based on the time it takes), or about one-third of the 2007 profits. Who would sign up for such "madness"; what benefits does it provide?

- ◆ *Happier, healthier, more present, more productive employees.*

- ◆ A *community* of employees, vendors, and customers who feel that they are being heard and in turn, because they are clear, they too listen with heightened awareness and sensitivity.

- ◆ *Empowered humans.* When we are getting cleared daily, over time we begin to understand that one's consciousness is the source of experience, that we are the one making it all up, that we can craft our lives in any way we choose.

The work force becomes more *attractive.* Customers and vendors want to be with our people. The experience of a clear space and clear people is a business magnet.

When employees are present they are *powerful and creative* because in the present is the only place creation exists.

Clear people are more *generous and grateful.* When you see that your experience is your creation, you are free. When you are free, you are looking less to the outer world for fulfillment. What naturally arises is thankfulness and the desire to serve.

Here is a sample of what our employees have said about getting cleared:

"The difference it has made is that I am given a chance to tell the truth every day, and in the truth lies freedom and I like freedom."

"Daily clearings have made such an impact on my life. I feel that they get me present to the choices I have. Each and every day I get to acknowledge how blessed my life is. I get to choose to step into service with a clear and open heart."

"It keeps me out of my head and in my heart."

"I get to connect with the person clearing me like I never knew was possible."

"I don't feel alone when I'm clear."

"Being able to say what is really going on for me, like the dark stuff we all hide from everyone, allows me to let it go and really live life full-out!"

"Before getting cleared I never thought about being present or about gratitude."

"I feel integrated in my work, like my whole self is present and being acknowledged."

"It quiets my mind. I get a break from all that mind chatter. I get to step out of myself and shine a light on who I am being and see if I want to change anything. It takes me out of unconsciousness. It gets me to see how great my life is and how great I am."

"Clearing has created the sacred space for honesty, integrity, mistakes, miscommunication, and judgment to have their own place without attachment or meaning."

"Clearing gives me the opportunity to connect on a deeper level with myself and spirit—dissipating the boundaries of separation."

"Being trained in clearing has allowed me to move through my own emotional states in a way that honors the experience I am having, without attachment to remaining in that place. I look forward to being cleared every day because I recommit to focusing on what is already working about my life, what is already going right, and how I am truly blessed in each moment."

"Before being cleared, I didn't quite know where to put my emotions, thoughts, judgments, and opinions. I felt stuck with them. I didn't understand that where I put my attention creates my experience. When I was able to practice this daily, I saw a dramatic shift in how I dealt with things that came my way. I began to experience being present, often, not only when life was 'going my way' but in the face of conflict."

Part of the experience we provide in the space we have sanctified is reverence. This reverence asks of our people a clear, present, and enrolled participation in the sacred act of service. The clearing removes much of the internal noise and collective static. Customers often comment on a discernable presence in Café Gratitude, the milieu of sacred space. If we didn't clear our people every day, we'd be just another restaurant serving food in exchange for money. For us the food, while vital, is subsidiary to the experience of communion. Perhaps that is why we are still in business and the world is demanding more of what we have to offer! Our society is hungry for meaning, fulfillment, healing, and connection. In Sacred Commerce we manage the being, and the being manages the doing. If your enterprise adopts clearing in its business model, your operation will be practicing Sacred Commerce.

HOW TO CLEAR

"It is in giving that we receive."

—FRANCIS OF ASSISI

1. Preparation begins with you. Get yourself cleared. This can be done with the first person you clear in the day.

2. "Be with" the person you are clearing, noticing any resistance to looking one another in the eyes. Just "be there," don't add anything. Take a breath together. That is the Sacred, Love, God, the Divine over there having another human experience. Be honored and honoring. If you are clearing by phone you can ask the person if they are ready and committed to being cleared.

3. Ask the person you are clearing what they are present to. There are many ways to express this query. Our district manager chooses a different question every day. The first questions deals

with the shadow, the wound. This question is designed to distinguish how the habitual mind is creating separation. It begins to cultivate an awareness that one's internal dialogue is a repetitive mechanism that tends to evoke fragmentation. Below are some of the questions we often ask, as the spirit moves us (you will find yourself offering others, according to circumstances and the experience of the moment).

- ◆ What are you present to?
- ◆ What is in the way of you being here right now?
- ◆ What version of "something's wrong" or "something's missing" are you listening to?
- ◆ What would you love to be forgiven for?
- ◆ What's your biggest disappointment?
- ◆ What's your biggest fear?
- ◆ Who do you gossip about?
- ◆ Where or with whom are you stingy?
- ◆ What are you resisting?
- ◆ How do you diminish yourself?
- ◆ Where are you being a victim in life?
- ◆ What past experience is still causing you suffering?
- ◆ Where are you not living up to your own standards?
- ◆ What failure has you stopped in your life?

If the person you are clearing stays conceptual or keeps talking about something other than their experience, ask them what that feels like. Example:

Clearer: "What are you present to?"
Being cleared: "My mother-in-law is coming tonight and my house is a wreck."

Clearer: "What I hear you saying is that your mother-in-law is coming tonight and that your house is a wreck." Now ask them: "How does that feel? What is that experience like?"

Being cleared: "I feel ashamed about my house and I'm afraid to be judged."

Clearer: "What I hear you saying is that you feel ashamed about the house and that you are afraid to be judged."

Now the one being cleared is more in their experience. They have moved from their head to their heart.

4. Listen/Recreation. Listen, don't fix. Recreate what the person being cleared said, verbatim, as in the preceding example. Let them know you got their communication. Let them be heard. The easiest way to derail a clearing is to try to fix the one being cleared. In the situation with the pending visit from the mother-in-law, if I had offered to send over a cleaning service, I would have validated the story that the one being cleared was living in. I would have moved their attention from their consciousness (something they have control over) to their circumstances. That would only deepen the illusion that life is about getting the conditions right. Trying to master the circumstances is the source of scarcity and suffering. Mastering being is the source of freedom. Do not coach during a clearing.

5. Creating something new. This question is an opportunity to shift one's attention to something new; to be present now, to love one's life. Here are some examples:

   ◆ What are you grateful for?

   ◆ What do you want to be acknowledged for?

   ◆ What do you love about your life?

   ◆ What is blessed about your life?

   ◆ What does your community love about you?

- ◆ What do you love about your parents (or mother-in-law)?
- ◆ What moves you?
- ◆ What inspires you?
- ◆ If money were no consideration, what would your life be for?
- ◆ Who has been a contribution to your life?
- ◆ What do you have an abundance of?
- ◆ In what way do you make a difference in the world?
- ◆ What do you love about this present moment?
- ◆ What is your life for?

6. Acknowledge the person being cleared. Thank them for being there, for their commitment to experience this bold adventure. Be moved, for when you are moved they are clear. This is perhaps the most important step, where a newfound freedom and connection with one another often occurs. Remember, there doesn't have to be evidence for acknowledgment. In speaking to the one being cleared, acknowledgment is the space that the clearer creates for the person being cleared to step into. The responsibility of the person doing the clearing is to dig deep, to be present to the contribution the employee is. This is not a rote process between management and employed. The clearing is an experience of vulnerability and openness moved by your witness to a fellow spiritual being sharing a profoundly human experience with you. Acknowledgment is calling forth the divine qualities in another that are already there, and in acknowledging them you both become present to them. The clearer, like a shaman, is a bridge between the visible and invisible worlds. If you are moved by the acknowledgment, you can be fairly confident the person you are sharing with is now clear, and love will be present.

To save time, clearing can happen in a group setting. The manager sits with the group, has people pair up, and takes them through the steps. The pairs clear each other. At the end of the clearing ask some of the employees to share with the group what they are present to now.

Clearing is a privilege. As employers of more than two hundred people, we see our mission as keeping people clear and inspired. If our people and the community we create together are inspired, the tasks encountered in our business day are filled with appreciation and a chemistry that makes work an expression of love.

PRACTICE

Start by clearing one other person and have him or her clear you. Do this daily—it is a practice. You will be amazed at how your ability to listen and hold space for others will grow. As you gain confidence, start clearing associates at work, especially those you manage.

5

The Calling of Mission Statements

Mission statements are an opportunity to align yourself, your employees, and your customer base with your commitments. It is most important that these statements are written in the present tense so as to always be current and happening now. The mission statement is a promise of what you will deliver as well as what you aspire to. When your people read it, their response is a big *yes*. There have been many times when one of our employees stands on top of a chair in the middle of a crowded café and asks everyone to pay attention as he or she reads our mission statement out loud. Imagine that happening in your business! What would your response be? I recall the first time this happened, I had to let go of any thoughts I had about the employee's spontaneity not being professional. I wondered where those thoughts of mine came from, and when I looked I saw that I had been taught that professionalism was not outspoken, but rather demure and reserved. I certainly could let that thought go, because now I see business as an opportunity to make a difference, to effect change, to speak out! Our customers typically love those moments when our statement is presented so spontaneously and with such passion by one of our employees. Many customers share that they hadn't really been aware of the depth of our mission; they had only heard about us from friends and wanted to experience Café Gratitude for themselves.

Just because you publish a mission statement does not signify that your customers know what it is, or that it is alive in the business. Look for opportunities to share your mission with others, and let people know who you are and what you stand for. Our employees feel free to communicate our stand in a very literal way. Our mission statement is a means for clearing our employees, for creating games for the business, as well as aligning our intentions as a community.

> **Cafe Gratitude** is our expression of a World of Plenty. Our food and people are a celebration of our aliveness. We select the finest organic ingredients to honor the Earth and ourselves, as we are one and the same. We support local farmers, sustainable agriculture, and environmentally friendly products. Our food is prepared with love. We invite you to step inside and enjoy being someone who chooses: loving your life, adoring yourself, accepting the world, being generous and grateful every day, and experiencing being provided for. Have fun and enjoy nourishing yourself.

PRACTICE

On an unmarked sheet of paper list the most important aspects of your mission. What do you aspire to? What is the example that inspires you, the flame that lights your heart and your path? Now take those and include them in a statement that challenges you to be bigger and brighter than you have thus far conceived of yourself. Continue to refine the statement until what you read inspires you. Remember to include the elements of the quadruple bottom line: Profit, Awakening, Sustainability, and Social Justice, or PASS.

6

Being as Source

"We don't see things as they are,
we see them as we are."

—ANAÏS NIN

In this huge, foolish project, "being" is what we are thinking, what we are saying to ourselves and others, what we believe, how we act, and what our attitude is. What we are thinking, speaking, believing, acting, and what concept or attitude we choose to adopt about our life creates our experience. Our life is who we are being about the conditions of our life. The condition of our business is who we are being about it. As noted, we estimate that it costs Café Gratitude LLC approximately $230,000 a year to clear our employees. If we "be" (think, speak, believe, act, and project the attitude) that the clearing is not worth the money or that employees don't appreciate the clearing, then we have created the experience of "something's wrong!" and we will experience fear and scarcity. We'll have won at the game we're playing called "something's wrong."

However, if we "be" (think, speak, believe, act, and project the attitude) that lives are being transformed during the clearings and our business is flourishing as a result, then we'll have created the experience of abundance and the feelings associated with making a difference. Where we invest our attention, our worship power, becomes our focus, that which we cultivate. As I sow, so shall I reap. Both scarcity and abundance are valid points of view. One is no more true or real than the other. They are both states of consciousness. Does an oak tree move you to tears of joy and appreciation, or is it an obstacle that stands in your way? What life do you choose to create with your attention? There is all the evidence necessary to conclude that the world is "going to hell in a hand basket," and that massive ecological breakdown is imminent. There is also ample evidence that humanity is awakening, and that our finest hour is at hand. Which is your world? Your belief makes it so.

> "There are three great mysteries:
> air to the bird, water to the fish, being to human."
> —ZEN SAYING

In Arizona, at age forty, I stood on the rim of the Grand Canyon for the first time in my life. All the years of anticipation could not prepare me for the magnitude of that vista. I was bowled over by its incredible and overwhelming beauty. About twenty feet away from me stood a man wearing an imposing belt buckle and a garish baseball cap. I overheard him announce to a female companion his reaction to the incomparable vista that lay before him: "You could dump garbage in there for a thousand years and you still wouldn't fill it up." He was having "his" Grand Canyon experience. Up until that moment, I thought we were all seeing the same canyon. Now I understand that all we ever see is "framed" by our thoughts, speech, beliefs, actions, and attitudes.

Living in the sacred is a choice, the chance to create every moment as an opportunity for awakening. How often do you squander that chance by turning your life into a "landfill" opportunity?

To what extent do you diminish yourself, your work, and your family with an unconscious, habitual view or interpretation?

Notice on any two days or at any two moments how our experience of our day can swing dramatically from peaceful to agitated, from fulfilled to unappreciated, from inspired to despairing. The circumstances are often the same, but who are we being about those circumstances? How we respond to them creates our experience. Have you ever been on vacation, surrounded by idyllic circumstances, and been miserable? Have you ever been unable to appreciate a beautiful sunset or enjoy your own children because of the clamor in your own head? Now ask yourself, have you ever been washing the dishes or scrubbing the mildew off the bathroom tile and found yourself fulfilled and "in the zone"?

As human beings we are always trying to manipulate the circumstances of our lives. All the while, it is who we are *being* about our life that gives us our life experience. Our whole traditional educational system is geared toward achievement—having, getting—while it is largely devoid of any training in being. The scarcity paradigm is all about having the "right" circumstances and then being happy and fulfilled. Notice the insatiable aspect of living life from outside-in. Our inherited view of life is to "get" this and then we can "be" that. Our society's massive advertising industry exists to fortify the "get this then be that" matrix. Ask almost anyone how their day was and they will likely speak about something that happened or a circumstance that occurred as the reason they are happy, disappointed, hopeful, fearful, and so forth. By taking on Sacred Commerce, one is stepping up to train one's self, one's co-workers, and associates to begin to master being. One takes on "being successful" without or before any evidence. This involves thinking, speaking, believing, acting, and having an attitude of success. A Sacred Commerce manager refrains from chasing

fulfillment in the outer. The sacred is here now, and that is where
the manager dwells.

In upstate New York in 1984, I was a father of two and, by de-
fault, a carpenter of C-minus quality. We lived hand to mouth.
When one job ended, the phone would ring with another prospect.
I deemed myself "spiritual" and professed that God provided just
enough, just in time. I was winning at the "just enough game."

Then a prosperity book came to my attention that gave me per-
mission to be spiritual and have money, and I took it on with a
vengeance. I started being a millionaire with no evidence. I drove
our $400 Saab automobile like a limo. I started to cherish money,
not for what it could buy, but for what it represented: the quality
of abundance that permeates all creation. I put Post-it notes
all around me that read, "I love money and money loves me." I
changed my name to Mighty Millionaire Matthew. Guess what?
Millionaire eventually showed up. At that time in my life, no one
would have placed bets on my fiscal prospects, but out of many
miraculous and unpredictable circumstances, I created a lucrative
fashion line and clothing factory in an old dairy barn in the Fin-
ger Lakes farm country, to the surprise and dismay of the grandees
of Seventh Avenue. My outer circumstances mirrored the shift in
my inner life, as they always do.

Is there any scientifically verifiable proof that my material world
shifted as a reflection of my being? No, there isn't. Rather, what I
undertook was an experiment in faith. Proof would require an
observer separate from the experience. In the "being game" you
are either all in, or not.

We can be grateful to countless fellow humans who have dem-
onstrated that life arises in who one is being, that being outshines
what we seem not to have or difficulties that have transpired in
our lives. Nelson Mandela, the gracious political prisoner of
apartheid, Ernest Shackleton, the Antarctic explorer of enduring

legend, and Mahatma Gandhi, India's beloved humanitarian activist, are three eminent examples of how the power of being is victorious over daunting circumstances and austere conditions. Elvis Presley, Judy Garland, and Howard Hughes are three examples of people for whom exalted circumstances, as evidenced in their acquisition and possession of wealth, talent, and success, guarantee nothing.

In the Buddhist view, life is neutral, and what we are thinking, speaking, believing, acting, and our attitude about life is all we ever actually experience. Why do we mostly have it backward? Why do we put so much emphasis on the doing, on managing the outer circumstances, on getting somewhere, and so little on being? This "backward" approach to life is the source of our scarcity experience. It's like looking at yourself in the mirror and trying to change the image you see by painting on the glass. No matter how much paint you apply to the mirror, there you are. Notice how we fill up our day doing something, getting something accomplished so we can be satisfied, like a deal we make with ourselves. What we check off as accomplished on our to-do list becomes our satisfaction meter. Consider that we can practice being satisfied and fulfilled Now!

In Sacred Commerce we take on the view that we can't fail because our mission—the transformation of the planet—is so herculean we can't be attached to the result. A transformed planet requires a transformed self. "Transformed" means continually giving up whatever is in the way of love. A Sacred Commerce manager is someone who is being present to love in every situation, who compassionately holds the space for the upset, the shadow, the resignation, the cynicism, the stormy weather to move through us and past us. One of our top managers set up an appointment to talk to us. She started sharing all her disappointments and incompletions, as we listened. She was speaking in a way that felt like she was making everything wrong, and yet she is highly trained to not be a victim of her circumstances. Eventually we heard how afraid she was, that she was being nudged from the inside by her own intuition to shift her focus and go more deeply into her spiritual training, and she was resisting it. She was afraid of letting go of what she had built with us. When we could simply be with her experience and let her share without reacting or defending, she was able to embrace her fears and see that what she wanted most was to step down to a lower level of management, making more room in her schedule to pursue her private spiritual training. We were able to support her moving beyond her fears into empowering her intuition, which is at the core of our work, so she no longer felt stuck and unappreciated.

We don't often look at it this way, but we can handpick what thoughts we have, how we speak, our beliefs, the actions we take, and the attitudes we entertain. They may seem automatic and they often are (try not thinking, or attempt to stay absolutely still for a long period of time), but those thoughts, words, and actions that we frequent, those that impact our lives, are the ones we've practiced to the point of becoming habitual. We are indulging in them, attending to them, and yet it appears to us that we "are" just that way. "I don't make enough money," "I'm not inspiring," "I'm not social," "I'm a klutz," "I'm too fat," "I'm unorganized," "I'm an addictive personality." These are statements and thoughts that we have practiced and mastered, thereby becoming for us our way of being. Consider that you can master any thoughts, any way of being.

One way to access mastery is through affirmation, which is just another method of repetition or practice. Affirmations are often perceived with cynicism as the inauthentic domain of New Age crystal-gazers. Consider that we are always affirming something.

"I'm a procrastinator" is an affirmation. "I'm shy" is an affirmation. "I'm not disciplined" is an affirmation. Do you question if these affirmations have an impact on your life? Are you cynical about their power over you? Notice that we only question the authenticity of the affirmations that create us as whole, complete, and loved. In one of the transformative workshops we share with others, a women said to me, "Affirmations are stupid and don't work."

"Really," I replied. "Are you a Mom?" I asked.

The woman nodded her head and replied, "Yes."

I said, "How often do tell yourself you could be a better Mom?"

She answered, "Oh, all the time."

"Does it work—do you create the experience of being a less-than-the-best Mom?" I queried.

"Oh!" she exclaimed in a moment of awakening.

The wound, the split, the shadow—in its effort to survive—wants us to believe we are broken. The wound seems real because it's more practiced and has been gathering a file of evidence on its behalf. Affirmation is a powerful and yet basic tool, accessible to everyone who can think or speak, for creating new files and new pathways to dispel the darkness and align us with love's presence, the sacred.

PRACTICE

Say out loud to yourself in the mirror, as follows:

"I love and honor myself as a divine creation."

"Love is having a [your name] experience."

"[Your name] is having a love experience."

"I adore myself."

7

Abundance Is an Inside Job

"Abundance can be had by simply consciously
receiving what has already been given."

—SUFI PROVERB

Abundance is a quality of the sacred, one of the flavors of the Oneness. How could anything be missing in a whole? Where would it be hiding? "Seek ye first the Kingdom of Heaven." First, be the Oneness, and abundance, joy, happiness, love, freedom, health, creativity, and all else will be given to you. This is our divine birthright. In fact, these qualities are always present, though we aren't always present to them. By "abundance" we mean "the assurance and knowledge of being supplied." By "supply" we mean resources that support our material existence: money, food, shelter, clothing, vacations, hot water, clean streets, verdant parks, music, tools, gasoline, transportation. It is easier for some of us to think of joy, love, and happiness as spiritual attributes, and it's often a bit of a stretch to think of an abundance of supply as a property of the divine.

Part of this training, this being Abundance, is living in the assurance of being supplied as a mindful practice that connects us to the sacred in everything. In being peaceful, we have peace. In being loving, our experience is love. In being joyful, we are present to joy. These qualities don't exist "out there."

Being Abundance is our access to experiencing Abundance—the faith that we are supplied; that the universe is hard-wired to furnish us with all our needs. The key to receiving this infinite storehouse of abundance is conscious gratitude for what you have already received and faith that you are going to receive more. Either individually or collectively as a work community, if we devote our attention to being supplied, the universe will mirror and be sculpted by our consciousness.

"To everyone who has, more will be given,
and he shall have an abundance;
but from the one who does not have,
even that which he has shall be taken from him."
—MATTHEW 25:29

The stock market and the economy are vivid demonstrations of this principle. The "value" of the nation's economy is beholden to our moment-by-moment consumer and investor confidence. The worth of a company or a property may vary greatly in any given day because of the collective public perception of its value, regardless of its authentic assets. Our collective experience of financial well-being is based on our ability to trust in the reality of our financial well-being. Trust and confidence are not bound by conditions—they're a matter of our attention. Look and see if your own prosperity barometer, your experience of economic fulfillment, is a function of the faith, confidence, and trust you have in yourself, your life, and our universe. Regardless of our circumstances, our balance sheet, our indebtedness, we propose that our moment-to-moment awareness of material well-being is a function of conviction and the barometer of our prosperity.

"Let us learn to think of dollars as we do leaves on trees, or oranges, as the natural and inevitable result of the law active within. There is truly no need to worry even when the trees appear to be bare, as long as we are conscious of the truth that the law is even now operating within to bring forth fruit after its own kind. Regardless of the state of our finances at any given moment, let us not be concerned or worried, because we know that the law acting in, through, and as our consciousness is at work within us, when we are asleep as well as when we are awake, to provide all those added things."

—JOEL GOLDSMITH, TWENTIETH-CENTURY MYSTIC

Let's briefly switch from a study of Abundance to the contemplation of Sacred Relationship to illustrate a point. For example, if you are trying to "get" a relationship, if your orientation is that love is "out there" like an external commodity to be acquired, you'll be left unfulfilled, even if you are in a relationship. Having a relationship is no guarantee of love. Having money doesn't guarantee the experience of abundance. Notice how the richest country in the world perceives that it still doesn't have enough "stuff," like oil. We'd apparently rather go to war to secure more stuff than practice being fulfilled by the assurance that there is always plenty for us.

For obvious reasons, the Tao of Abundance is a Sacred Commerce practice. At Café Gratitude we have eight general managers who are paid the same salary. Those who really take on "being" rich are just that. Their experience is that they are provided for, therefore they're much less consumed by their individual survival paradigm and consequently are free to serve our company's mission and enjoy their lives. They are more present to and for the whole community—they are our best managers. In any enterprise, managers who present and invoke abundance as an inner quality are a huge asset. The flavor of abundant leadership is that there is no place to get and nothing to prove; life is here and now, and anything is possible.

> "By letting go it all gets done.
> The world is won by those that let go,
> but when you try and try,
> the world is beyond winning."
> —LAO TZU

The only failure would be to make failure signify something. Life already turned out superbly, so a manager steeped in the sacred blesses every dollar and plays the game of business full-out. Customers, employees, and vendors are inspired by the freedom of their non-attachment and want to participate fully in the enterprise. Imagine a business where everyone is developing abundance consciousness and holds each other accountable for being the source of their supply. How might a work community improve if we held each other and our lives as whole and complete in the process of awakening?

We are present to the radical consciousness that this belief represents. If abundance is an inside job, if the experience of being provided for is a quality of the sacred that is always available within us, if security can't be found in the outer, then what is the point of business? Remember, commerce is a vehicle for the sacred to take shape, form, and substance. Business is an expression of love, a school of transformation, a game of making a difference. Now you can play it with conscious intention. There is no place to get, nothing to prove, and failure doesn't mean what you thought it did. Now you get to live the extraordinary life of a merchant priest, a director of consciousness, a managing partner for God.

PRACTICE

Have managers practice with each other and with employ-ees. Say this eleven times to a partner and then switch, so your partner can say it to you: "I am giving up wants I no longer need. I am completely fulfilled in this *now* moment."

8

The Manager as Coach

"This is the true joy in life. The being used for a purpose recognized by yourself as a mighty one. The being a force of nature instead of a feverish, selfish little clod of ailments and grievances complaining that the world will not devote itself to making you happy. I am of the opinion that my life belongs to the whole of the community, and as long as I live, it is my privilege to do for it whatever I can. I want to be thoroughly used up when I die, for the harder I work, the more I live. I rejoice in life for its own sake. Life is no 'brief candle' to me; it is a sort of splendid torch which I have got hold of for the moment, and I want to make it burn as brightly as possible before handing it on to future generations."

—GEORGE BERNARD SHAW

There is a new shaman in town. Gourd rattles and sage smoke are optional, but vision and commitment are not. Sacred Commerce managers are the stewards of consciousness for a business. Like the seat of wisdom held by tribal elders, they steer the community toward the sacred. They hold that seat even if the stormy weather of doubt, separation, and scarcity rolls through an enterprise. While the collective shadow clings to appearances—

sub-par forecasts for first-quarter earnings, a pending lawsuit, a glitch in production—the new merchant priests and priestesses use their tools to keep the sacred space clear, moving toward One-ness. They lean into the discomfort, asking hard questions like: What would love do now? What master are we serving? Is it love or fear I'm speaking with? They shore up themselves and the company culture, focusing attention on the mission statement and continually asking themselves, "Are we a PASS?"

- ◆ Are we Profitable? Does it serve the company as an entity?
- ◆ Are we Awakening? Does this cause transformation?
- ◆ Are we Sustainable? Are we in harmony with the Earth?
- ◆ Are we Serving? Are we creating a just society?

Like any initiate, the Sacred Commerce manager's life is a continuous act of surrender. This merchant priest lives in the paradox between emptiness, knowing nothing, and being a warrior of daring action. Their impossible promise to a transformed world is so extremely challenging and highly inspiring that their personal wants and habitual shadows have less sway over them.

The manager's business is humanity's business, and businesses become schools of transformation. Sacred Commerce managers are actively transforming life. They are activists. They make a stand for a sustainable world committed to love and fulfillment awakening in the hearts of all humankind. They live the possibility of being present and mastering the now moment. They live like there is no place to get to. Notice how much of our suffering comes from feeding the "hungry ghost" and trying to find fulfillment in the outer world. To be insatiable (not enough money, time, beauty, love, etc.) is to validate and participate in the collective fear factor that breeds scarcity and selfishness, the source of war, hoarding, and indifference.

For the Sacred Commerce manager, adversity is an ally and conflict an opportunity. They are masters at holding space while the shadow moves through. They are the first to be transparent, apologize, and take 100% of the responsibility. Putting the collective interests before their personal comfort zone, they attend to the building of a community. The medicine this new shaman carries and administers is the healing salve of *distinctions*. Distinctions distinguish and support our attention; they differentiate fear from love. Distinctions are not the truth but rather are like different pairs of spectacles, each with a view to try on and determine if the vista they provide empowers and heals. The Sacred Commerce manager does not traffic in the truth; he or she is a coach inviting employees to look in a different way and discover for themselves the face of love.

PRACTICE

Look at your business or the business you are involved in. If you were being 100% responsible for the condition of the business, if the business is an out-picturing of your consciousness, what can you be responsible for? Who are you being such that business conditions are that way?

This is a great practice for yourself and all managers.

When we are closing out the month's financials with our managers, we ask them who they were being such that the month turned out the way it did. Win or lose, how is it a result of who you were being?

This practice allows managers to see where they get stopped, where they break through, where there is room for growth, setting them up to powerfully enter the new month.

9

Manager Medicines: Distinctions

t is not necessary that a Sacred Commerce manager master these distinctions, only that they try them on, practice them, and bring them to the community. In giving them away, one anchors them in one's practice. We often practice a distinction as a community in our various meetings (see Chapter 10, entitled "Leading Inspiring Meetings"). A Sacred Commerce manager has no answers. Rather, we are always asking the community to look and see what may be in the way. The distinctions are a reminder that life, as well as commerce, is an inside job. If the business community is present and grateful for the abundance of their collective and individual lives, the business will flourish regardless of outer circumstances.

Does that mean there won't be breakdowns? Of course not. Remember: challenges are opportunities to move through some resistance, to restore integrity. Challenges are guides, like rocks in the river steering the current toward the ocean. The rocks will get larger; the challenges will become worthy of your life and the life of the community. As a business steps more and more out of survival consciousness (survival of the individual or business), what naturally arises is the desire to serve the whole.

Abundance: the presence, knowingness, and assurance of being supplied. Money is its outer expression; however, money is not abundance. Kisses are an outer expression of love, but kisses are not love. Abundance is an inner quality, a presence like love.

Acknowledgment: the tool to address and elicit divine qualities in employees, customers, owners. It is our attention actualized: seeing the best and giving voice to that sight by acknowledging qualities of the divine, thereby inviting that presence into consciousness.

Affirmations: create new files, new patterns in being that align one with the sacred.

Anatomy of an upset: understand that upsets are not personal. They are akin to inclement weather moving across the landscape—in this case, through a person or a community. There is usually one or more of four elements at play in an upset: 1) a reminder of an earlier, similar incident; 2) a perception of thwarted intention; 3) an unfulfilled expectation; 4) an undelivered communication.

Apology: the premier sign of being responsible, an act of generosity and surrender. It communicates that one is more invested in kindness than in being right. Apology softens attitudes and dissolves lines of separation while restoring love. We say a leader always apologizes first and takes 100% responsibility.

Being: we experience being through our thoughts, speech, beliefs, actions, and attitudes. Master being and you master your life experience.

Being with: to be with another without goals or expectations, to look them in the eyes without speaking, without adding or subtracting anything, to "be" there for and with them.

Breakthrough: something becomes possible that wasn't possible before a piece of the past (some limiting view) is removed from the present.

Clearing: creating a blank canvas of the present moment, free of anxieties about the future and constraints of the past. Clearing is a technique for having employees be here now.

Enrollment: when you enroll others, what you communicate manifests not as a dogmatic edict or an order from on high, but as an opportunity for them.

Failure: we perceive failure as a sliver of our experience, nothing more; as not doing what one promised to do in the time one committed to do it. That's it! Everything else that is labeled "failure," along with the heavy guilt trip that society lays on it, is just story, noise, static.

Forgiveness: to sincerely give as you gave before. To take measures to restore love in any relationship. To really understand that there is nothing to forgive.

Four Insights for Sacred Commerce: 1) Be the space for all of it. 2) Create a sacred place. 3) Be in the game. 4) Be an invitation.

The Game: creating business as a game, reaching financial or other business goals through games that inspire you and your employees. Creating some context that lights you up on a day-to-day basis.

Generate: we are the source of our experience. We can generate any experience. Being happy is a practice, being sad is a practice; we can choose, so choose something that empowers your business. The hugging saint of India, Amma, generates a huge welcome and goodwill to all of humanity through the simple feat of giving hugs to thousands of people a day.

Getting complete: to declare that any past disturbance is no longer impacting the present. Being complete means there is a clear loving space between you and another.

Gossip: to diminish another with our speech, or to listen to another diminish someone with their speech. Since there is no "other," gossip ultimately diminishes ourselves and the community.

Hold space: to stay in the seat of love and compassion while the storm of the shadow, the angst of separation, moves through an individual or community.

I made a mistake! To be human is to make mistakes. If we are not making mistakes we are playing a really small game. To declare "I made a mistake" when you have is a game that a business plays to create a shame-free environment. See the section on "Creating Games" (Chapter 25).

I'm making up . . . : this is a way of communicating that makes you responsible for the story you are creating, acknowledging that it is not the truth. This allows room for others to see what stories they are creating. For example: "I'm making up that you don't want to be here today." "I'm making up that you are upset with me."

Integrity: being your word, doing what you say you are going to do by the time you said you were going to do it, and when you are not going to deliver, communicate and re-promise. This creates workability for yourself and the community.

Internal dialogue: the habitual disempowering chatter, static, and noise in one's head.

Language of Oneness: speaking in a way that presences Oneness. Example: "It's my job that you win at your job—what can I do for you?" or "I'm having the experience that you are not enjoying your job—do you have any requests of me?"

Lifelines: techniques that intervene in any habitual experience of limitation. Lifelines extract us from the clutches of ego's internal dialogue of "something's wrong, something's missing."

> *Lifeline 1.* Laughing out loud for one minute for no reason.
>
> *Lifeline 2.* Giving something away: time, money, some form of supply, or acknowledgment.
>
> *Lifeline 3.* Telling someone what you are grateful for or asking someone what they are grateful for. Asking the question of the day.
>
> *Lifeline 4.* Practicing affirmations in the mirror or with a partner.

Listening: the highest form of loving. There are multiple levels of listening. The highest is conscious listening, which can liberate the storyteller from the story. One of the loftiest compliments our society pays a human being is to say that she or he is a "good listener." A Sacred Commerce manager uses listening as a way to empower employees and gain their trust by being in their world and not trying to fix or change it.

Love is granting being: love is honoring everyone's journey, everyone's awakening, equally.

Loving money: money is an expression or representation of the divine presence of abundance that is everywhere, always. Money represents the inner quality of abundance, the knowingness of always being provided for. In the same way, a photograph of your children (loved ones) represents the inner quality of love.

Making a difference: being a contribution as a path of surrender and awakening to the whole; giving over your life to being of service to the whole; no longer serving just your individual wants, desires, and comforts.

Making requests: when you become powerful at making requests you are unstoppable. A manager powerful in making requests can build leadership and team spirit without domination. This is an alternative to making demands. Making requests builds and demonstrates self-worth and self-loving. A community that is powerful in making requests has a high level of workability because everyone's intentions or desires are clear, and people can readily be supported.

Money as a sacrament: money is a fluid that circulates through the body of humanity. Money doesn't go anywhere. Every time money changes hands it is a sacred opportunity to connect, to acknowledge our interconnectedness, our Oneness. Money is a representation of the divine attribute of abundance.

Non-attachment: giving, living, loving, full-out, 100%, without expectations. Expectations suck the joy out of life.

Nothing is personal: they are not responding to you. Their upset, their actions are not about you. Freedom lies here, within.

Perfect: One creator, One creation, One awakening. What about the Grand Canyon is not perfect? Consider that an evolving process is perfect. Your business, your employees, the Earth ...

Question of the day: a Sacred Commerce manager has more questions than answers. Their questions elicit Oneness for employees, customers, vendors, and owners. What are you grateful for?

Recreation: a tool for verifying that the person being listened to has been heard. "Recreation" in this sense means to re-create what the other person said, to narrate back to the person speaking what you heard from them, verbatim, thus making certain they understand that you heard them.

Recurrent: a re-occurring and habitual story of limitation: "I'm shy." "I should have gone to college." "They're fickle." "Spiritual people are too spaced out." "I can't find good help." "My wife doesn't listen." "My boss is a jerk." "I'm not that intelligent." "We should have outsourced Human Resources." These are the crippling stories about ourselves and our world that we cause to recur in our thoughts and words, thereby inhibiting the ever-present, limitless potential for creation of the new, which is the gift and promise of Life and Oneness, Love and Fulfillment. Grab a lifeline, not a storyline.

Sacred service: serving the whole community as a path of awakening. It is seeing service as a way to transcend the domination of the small self.

Scarcity: the human condition of telling ourselves "there is not enough"—not enough time, money, beauty, love, health, energy, and intelligence. Scarcity is the illusory condition that we create while surrounded by the reality of a universe of abundance.

Supply: the resources that support our material existence—money, food, transportation, medicine, shelter, fuel, education, etc.

There is nothing wrong: "wrong" is a costly label. In Oneness there is only love and our resistance to love. Concepts of "right and wrong" retard the individual as well as the community by getting us stuck in a "position." Dwelling in right or wrong or blame is a distraction. Instead ask yourself, "What would love do now?"

Transformation: getting the past complete, out of the present. Transformation is to be inspired by the empty blank canvas of the present moment, to be moved by a new possibility free of past constraints and habits.

Whole and complete: we are whole and complete when we see that there is nowhere to get and nothing to prove, that our value is already established by virtue of our sacred creation. Our obsession with "fixing" ourselves obstructs our way of experiencing our perfection and expressing love.

PRACTICE

Pick one of the above distinctions. Read it out loud at a meeting with your co-workers and ask them to share what they hear and how they could apply it.

10

Leading Inspiring Meetings

W e view our meetings as opportunities to clear, educate, and inspire our people. We see these gatherings as the calling of a sacred circle, a council of powerful and insightful beings. We start all our meetings with an inspiring group clearing, making sure that we all address what is currently surfacing in the company. For example, if employees are starting to show up late for work, our clearing is about integrity. Or if we are having a cash shortage issue, our clearing is about caring for the one being, and how much we are an interactive part of one another's lives. We always clear them by asking for a volunteer to be publicly cleared, after which we pair everyone else up for the group clearing. In this way the space is set and the clearing can go deeper.

At first, we ourselves led all meetings, all individual café operations, all guidance and oversight of managers and employees. As we grew and advanced our people into management, further training them in "holding space" and "enrollment," their growth empowered us to step away from the individual café operations and, most recently, even from our managers' meetings.

"Holding space" and effecting "enrollment" are essential to leading inspiring employee meetings. It is necessary to be able to maintain the attention of the whole on the big picture, our mission, while speaking to issues directly. Enrollment is the ability to have what you're saying occur as an opportunity for others, to enroll them in what is possible. We look upon our meetings as inspirational trainings, and the job of our General Managers is to keep their staff inspired.

All Café Gratitude meetings are opportunities to realign ourselves with our mission statement. We make it a priority to create and go over the agendas for meetings, as well as to clear the managers who will be leading portions of the meeting. This is a wonderful opportunity for employees to develop their speaking and listening skills and to be inspired and inspiring. Anyone can contribute to the agenda by submitting a subject or issue in advance. This helps us address issues that everyone is dealing with and want addressed as a whole. We are committed to ensuring that if our people are going to be attending meetings, they get their life out of being there. We request that the managers come early and start the meeting by welcoming each person as we want them to welcome our customers. We serve them coffee or tea with the same devotional service we expect of them. In short, the meeting should be well worth them getting up at 7 a.m. for. We've discovered that it is better to handle discussion of chores and minute details concerning job assignments at smaller meetings geared for specific departments, while keeping the larger work-community meetings focused on the big picture and what truly brings and keeps us together.

One of the primary benefits of meetings is the opportunity they afford the managers to lead by realigning themselves with the vision. Business-as-usual and work-as-habit can cause us to lose sight of why we are called together. Prosaic day-to-day operations can, if we are not aware of the process, sometimes obstruct our broader vision and our implementation of that vision in the inspiration of this moment that we are creating. Our challenge is to keep the radiant fire burning in our hearts and those of our associates, vendors, and customers. Remember, if you aren't inspired, they won't be either. We always close our meetings standing in a friendly and welcoming circle and sincerely sharing acknowledgment of one another. The emphasis here is on sincerity, by which we invest our gatherings with the sacred and with unconditional love, without which they could become a mere going-through-the-motions habit. The higher your aspiration, the more you have to invest in keeping it real and spontaneous. Your employees should truly feel that you do not desire that their participation be a mimic of what is perceived as the response desired by the employer. Rather, through the example of the business owner's personal integrity and commitment to living the life of the sacred merchant moment to moment, cynicism and doubts dissolve. The reality of a higher model of commerce is presented to your people as an invitation to share in the adventure of actualizing the dream of happier and holier models of life, work, and prosperity, through service that we make sacred.

GUIDELINES FOR INSPIRING MEETINGS

- The context is a sacred circle or gathering.
- Start with an inspiring clearing.
- Be enrolling—what you say occurs as an opportunity. Be willing to be vulnerable and transparent; share what is really there for you.
- Hold your seat, be willing to hear whatever may be shared, don't make anything wrong.
- One person speaks at a time and starts with "I love and honor myself and I am happy to share myself with you." The others respond, "We love and honor you and are happy to listen to you with love."
- Everyone may contribute to the agenda.

◆ Start on time, end on time.

◆ Always include some element of education.

◆ Always include some element of challenge or growth.

◆ Idea: you can always take one of the Manager Medicines and focus the meeting on furthering the understanding and application of that distinction.

◆ Presence the miraculous.

◆ End with acknowledgment.

11

The Art of Sacred Service

grew up in the food business. My mother was always preparing and serving food. It was the focal point of her life. My first job was in a hospital kitchen as a dietician's assistant. Later I worked in restaurants, managed restaurants, founded a wholesale bakery, and catered private parties. In my years of recovery I broke away from the hospitality industry and began a greeting card company, as well as selling cosmetics. I love serving people. One night when I was in my mid-forties, after a challenging shift at a local restaurant, I returned home thinking, why am I still doing this? When is it going to be my turn to be waited on? That night I had a dream that Jesus (whom I love and grew up studying) came to me and asked me to serve at The Last Supper. When I awoke the next morning I had a whole new context for service. I saw that while it would have been great to attend The Last Supper, my true vocation was to serve it. This is the highest calling and the mark of a true leader: to be the servant of all. I am honored to be of service. I remember how, in the early days of the café, I could be joyful while cleaning out the strainer baskets in the produce sink, looking out at the customers and managers in the more glamorous front of the house, for no matter what I was doing I was sure that all there was to do was be of service.

Sacred service occurs when we get our selves out of the way. That is one reason why our clearing practice is so valuable. When employees have their attention on the details, breakdowns, or circumstances of their lives, it is difficult for them to be here, now, fully in service to our customers. We're not advising you to ignore the circumstances of your employees; we are counseling you to empower them by training them to be present, which is the only place anyone has any power to create anything.

Sacred service entails seeing yourself as an expression of the divine, the one being, the source of all life and love. When you see yourself as love, all there is to do is serve. Love is only experienced when it is shared or given away. Serving is an extension, an expression of love—love moving through us, out into the world.

PRACTICE

Where in your work experience are you feeling obligated, stuck, or unappreciated? If you took on being a conduit of love and recognize that this situation is an opportunity for providing sacred service, what do you suppose your experience might be? What if every contact at work was simply an opportunity to presence love? What if you were known at work as the person who loved everyone?

12

There Is Nothing Wrong

Most of us have grown up in a culture where there is definitely something wrong when things do not turn out the way we expect them to. If it wasn't that way for us at home, it most likely was that way at school. Consciously or unconsciously, we have been acculturated to believe that there is a way that life should be, and if it isn't that way, there is something wrong with us, with those around us, and with life itself. Letting go of this concept can be challenging, for we have also come to believe that change occurs when something is so wrong we can no longer stand it. We want you to consider that there is power in realizing that change can be initiated at any time, and nothing needs to be "wrong" in order to actualize change.

Consider this: you could change a job or a relationship that is in great shape. It isn't a prerequisite that something needs to be in bad shape in order for you to move on. Making something or someone wrong diminishes you and your life; it places you in judgment of someone or something and separates you from the unity of life. Only when we are one with the whole of life can we know ourselves as fulfilled and complete, missing nothing. Many people spend their lives looking to complete themselves through accomplishment. What if the only true completion is when we come to know ourselves as one with all of life, with no separation or judgment?

Some people imagine that the flip-side of "nothing is wrong" is resignation to a set of circumstances. That is not what we are saying. We are advocating standing for what you believe, creating business as an opportunity to initiate powerful change in the world, including the awakening of its people, and a good starting place is the vision that there is nothing wrong.

I recall an occasion in which an employee contacted us feeling angry and unappreciated. In the face of this expression, I reflexively began to wonder why we were working so hard to keep this person on board. I started thinking, 'This is a waste of time.' I caught myself and shifted my attention to all the ways in which the employee had contributed to our company. I also thought about the beneficial difference we have made in the employee's life. My judgment separated me from the win-win we had been for each other, the awakening process we were sharing. We could learn and grow from being in relationship; this person was actually contributing to us, in part by flushing out my impatience. When I let go of my inclination toward making the employee wrong, I immediately felt connected and appreciative.

PRACTICE

Identify a situation at work where you are creating the belief that "there is something wrong; it shouldn't be this way." Now consider what the impact of that view is on the quality of your life. Ponder an outcome in which you let go of the idea that there's something wrong and instead just see that this is the way that situation is—what would your experience be? What might you be feeling? What actions might you take?

13

Giving Up Being Right

Consider the fact that as human beings we are nearly addicted to "being right." How many times do you find yourself arguing from some position you aren't even that committed to? Consider that what there is to transform is being kind instead of being right. The Dalai Lama of Tibet says, "My religion is kindness."

In being right there is no workability, only positions to defend. We actually train our managers to apologize first and take 100% responsibility. We practice this in our own lives as well. This is the place to stand that gives freedom and power. Every situation is an opportunity to awaken: to our commitments, to our healing, to our expressions of separation, to whatever might be in the way of our experiencing Oneness. When we can let go of our need to be right we are able to connect and work with others, rather than spend all our energy defending our view or position.

When we opened the first Café Gratitude we provided natural linen aprons for our employees; however, they didn't hold up well and showed stains easily. So we switched to black aprons. It wasn't long after that when employees started saying that they didn't like the aprons. Managers met with us and we explored a variety of uniform options. We invited the employees to present their thoughts and ideas. A uniform was a big step for us since our employees tend toward individuality, thinking in new ways, being activists. When we devised a uniform we presented it at the all-employees meeting. There was definitely some resistance. Within weeks they had creatively modified their uniforms with slits, staples, and pins. We requested, however, that they all empower what we had chosen and thanked them for their input and participation. We've gone with that uniform for almost a year now, and most recently the employees came to us saying that the aprons are too long and restrict their ability to move easily. So we took their advice and have now devised a shorter apron. This is a great example of our letting go of some way we thought it should be and instead really working with our staff to create a solution together. Sure, this took some time, but had we just designated a uniform and been "right about it," or made our people wrong for being so individualistic, we would have spent so much more time trying to defend our position and the policy, and perhaps lost some really great people in the process who were also being so right about their view that they could not have continued to work with us. Some of those employees have a renewed commitment to Café Gratitude having experienced being partnered with and heard.

PRACTICE

Interact with another person by discussing the following: What is a position you have about your company that you aren't willing to let go of? What does that position cost you (what's the impact on your life)? Share with a partner. Now share with your partner what you see would be available (what would fill that space) if you were to let go of that position.

14

The Power of Making Requests

M aking requests is an important aspect of powerful leadership. Historically, leaders often end up feeling taken for granted, overworked, and underappreciated. We don't have a strong cultural belief that others want for us what we want for ourselves, and so we may think it is necessary, maybe even noble, to go without. But that limit is not necessary in Sacred Commerce, where we celebrate one another, where we want for others what we want for ourselves.

One of our managers wanted to go to Hawaii but rather than come to our meeting and request the time off, she bought a ticket and then presented it as "I already have my ticket so I need to get the time off." We supported her in seeing that she not only diminished her experience of being supported and celebrated by her management team, but she diminished their experience of being people who would of course want her life to be great and would alter their schedules to make her trip happen. She created a prerequisite and then made her request because she did not trust us to grant it without it.

What normally stops people from making powerful requests is either not feeling worthy, or the fear of someone in authority saying no. Remember that "no" just signifies "not right now." Any other significance attached to it is baggage that has been added:

"They don't like me." "I never get what I want." "They think I'm selfish." "They don't appreciate all the work I do for them." Requests are opportunities for others to contribute to you. This is where being worthy enters the mix. If you aren't able to receive a contribution without feeling indebted, or doubting yourself, you may get inhibited when considering making the request. Making requests is a valuable and necessary element of building a healthy community and company.

PRACTICE

With a partner, practice making a request that is a stretch for you, one that is normally difficult for you to make. Your partner is going to say no. Make the request again; again your partner is going to say no. Continue to do this until you start to realize that "no" doesn't mean anything except "not right now." Switch and repeat the practice, having your partner making the request.

15

The Gift of Acknowledgment

Consider that there is no such thing as acknowledging someone too much. Culturally we are more critical of ourselves and others than we are generous. Acknowledgment is an act of generosity. We aren't talking about acknowledging someone because of anything; we are saying that an acknowledgment can be generated from nothing. Mostly in life we acknowledge people for something they have done or something we can experience. We are saying that to acknowledge is to bring forth something, to elicit, to call into being. For example, I might acknowledge an employee for being courageous, creating them as courageous in the face of their job. This doesn't mean that they have already done a courageous act; it means that I am calling them forth to be courageous since I have just shared with them that I see them that way.

You probably have heard about the school teacher who was given a classroom full of learning-challenged students. The teacher was told that these students had high IQs. With this assumption, in the course of the experiment their scores on intelligence tests increased. By the same token, consider the teacher who was given a classroom full of very bright students but was informed that they had mediocre IQ scores—over the span of the experiment their score on intelligence tests dropped, based on the lowered expectations that the teacher had and mirrored for the students.

When we acknowledge qualities of intelligence or divinity in others, those qualities manifest. That is the magic of acknowledgment! We aren't saying that you manipulate your people: do this to get that. We are saying to truly acknowledge them from your heart, with love. See that they are *already* those qualities, and that your inability to see those qualities is a block in the flow. When we take on acknowledging them, we too begin to see what we are looking for. This is a powerful practice in seeing the best in others. When you acknowledge something, it shows up because it was already there; you just couldn't see it because you weren't acknowledging it! Qualities of the divine are always present in each of us— they can't not be, it's just that we may not be present to them. Acknowledgment is the practice of getting ourselves present to those qualities in others and in ourselves.

PRACTICE

Practice with another person. Practice acknowledging your partner for any quality of the divine: being courageous, beautiful, peaceful, joyous, worthy, loving, etc. Really let yourself get present to how extraordinary he or she is. Practice this until you can see and feel the quality you are calling forth. Next, practice asking for acknowledgment. With your partner, ask to be acknowledged for something you would love to be acknowledged for and practice really embracing the truth of the acknowledgment. Now switch and let your partner request to be acknowledged. Acknowledgment is bringing out the best in one another.

16

The Value of Integrity

We don't interpret integrity as being good or bad. Integrity is the quality of being whole, undivided, complete. This is being attentive to a workability for all. It has been our observation that at the core of any failure there is an "out-of-integrity." This is a key distinction in the growth or development of a business. We watch for any loss of integrity in our company; this includes with our people. For example, we discovered on one occasion that a manager had omitted writing up an employee as part of a disciplinary action. The manager felt that sufficient amends had been made; the manager was short-staffed and didn't want to create additional pressure to get shift positions filled. The issue with that attitude is that word got out about the oversight, and some other employee who had been disciplined according to protocol was now disgruntled and felt unfairly treated. There was also a tendency for employees to relate to other policies with the attitude that there may be exceptions and loopholes in those as well. As a result, the organizational system begins to crumble; our integrity was out. When we work with and train our managers, we share with them our approach to integrity as signifying doing what you said you would do, when you said you would do it. The corollary to that is communication: if you aren't going to fulfill your commitment, get in communication and clean it up, and then commit on the basis of your new promise. This process builds trust and workability for all.

There was another occasion when we had shortages in cash occurring on a fairly regular basis. At the next all-employees meeting we discussed this and shared how important our integrity is. We talked with our employees about how, when there is a blatant out-of-integrity such as cash missing, everyone suffers: suspicion sets in, innocent employees begin to grow anxious wondering if managers suspect them; people no longer feel free to talk about their finances in case someone interprets their financial situation as a need for money and maybe an inducement for taking it. Everyone begins to mistrust everyone else. We let our employees know that we were committed to restoring the integrity. We made a request of the community for whoever it was to please come to us and clean it up, restore their integrity. We also shared that we viewed this theft as an out-of-integrity for the community; who were we being that someone was living with such desperation and we didn't know about it? We promised not to terminate anyone's employment; we related that we saw the situation as a cry for love and wanted to be able to support the person involved. At the time, no one unburdened themselves and came forward, but the misappropriation of the cash ceased. Months later, when two different workers chose to leave our employ, both cleaned up admirably and admitted that they had taken from us in the past. They sincerely apologized.

Consider a larger perspective: many of us are increasingly aware of the impact that our diet has on the planet. A meat-based diet is resource-intensive, requiring massive amounts of land, water, grain, and fossil fuels. Farm animal metabolism is one of the top sources of greenhouse gases, yet we go on eating meat. You could call this an out-of-integrity—people are starving, resources are diminishing, life on this planet is threatened, and yet meat continues to be heedlessly consumed in vast quantities. Are we not also part of this cycle? We may not be consuming meat every day, but we are always at the impact of our choices. Look at how we live in a state of defending our personal boundaries: my car, my parking space, my food, my house, my children. Notice how this plays out in the world, with 80% of our tax revenues spent "defending" ourselves, our borders, our right not to share. There is a cost to our quality of life even now, from either living at a level of unconsciousness or numbing ourselves to the impact others are experiencing due to the choices we are making. Where is the workability for the whole?

We are not accusing. We view all breaks in the continuum of integrity as opportunities for growth and healing. Some may think us hopelessly naive for regarding the missing cash at our café as a cry for love and help from the persons culpable. But who truly is naive in such a scenario? We have come to accept that hardening ourselves is part of the fashionably cool facade that successful people are encouraged to cultivate. Out-of-integrity reveals a fragmentation, and fragmentation is crying for unity-with-whole. We have worked hard to refrain from making an out-of-integrity a good or bad judgment. It is just a break in the wholeness, and an opportunity to reconnect and commune openly with the one struggling. Being alert to opportunity is a truism in Business 101, but how many in business are alert to out-of-integrity as opportunity? The love you demonstrate to all is the business of sacred commerce.

PRACTICE

Share with a partner a recent break in your own integrity. How did you justify it; what was the cost to you or your company? Then share what you are willing to take on to restore your integrity: write a letter, make a phone call, have a straight conversation, forgive yourself.

17

Looking at Upsets

W e have a way of looking at upsets that supports people in defusing them. Many of us go around avoiding upsets—evading anger, confrontation, disappointment, and worry. We on the other hand say that upsets are opportunities to heal, connect, and remember. Instead of backing away from or avoiding an upset, if we take it apart we will find that one or more of the following characteristics exists in the upset, and in spotting these characteristics we have more facility and power with the upset.

- ◆ What is upsetting you reminds you of a similar experience from the past.
- ◆ You have an intention that is thwarted.
- ◆ You have an expectation that is not fulfilled.
- ◆ You have something to communicate that you have not delivered.

When you can look at an upset and see what is at play within it, it is possible to relate to it quite differently. If you are the one who is experiencing the upset, can you see that the upset is always with you, that you are the one who is experiencing the suffering? Notice that you are the one with the unfulfilled expectation, the thwarted intention, undelivered communication, or regret from the past.

Can you see if you are with someone who is experiencing an upset that they are not responding to you, that the upset is with them? They are now the one who is suffering, the one with the unfulfilled expectation, thwarted intention, undelivered communication, or past regret. Please note: if you have any reaction to someone's upset, this is now your upset, equal opportunities to heal, to get complete, to become one. As managers we affirm that it is our responsibility to let upsets move through like weather. This is a sacred position and an honorable responsibility of management: to simply let the upsets be, to support your people in seeing them through new eyes, and to begin to have power around them. This is the holding of sacred space, trusting the process of awakening.

Upsets aren't "bad." We're all working through our blockages, getting our lessons, healing old wounds. Upsets are our allies, our true being showing us where we are creating separation, where we aren't being one. They are an opportunity to expand our small selves into the infinite oneness we are.

One day a manager asked one of our servers if she would set up a table. The server replied something along the lines of "Does it look like I'm not doing anything?" The manager replied graciously, "What did you hear me say?" and at that point the server stopped and got present to how out of context and filtered her response had been, how much she had added to the manager's simple request. Had she initially responded, "I heard you say you want me to set up that table like I'm not busy already." Then the manager would have had an opportunity to either clarify the simplicity of her request or clean up and apologize for speaking to her in a diminishing way, seeing her as less than fully participating.

PRACTICE

Make a request of a partner/co-worker. Have your partner react as in an upset. Then you reply, "What did you hear me say?" and let your partner respond. This is a powerful exercise in how what we say is heard through the filters of one another and often misinterpreted. This elementary exercise allows each of us to truly hear what is being said and note how often we add something to it that creates an upset. It also allows the person speaking to clean up what shows up in the unsaid, if applicable. Now switch and practice again.

18

Getting Complete with Failure

"I've missed more than nine hundred shots in my career. I've lost almost three hundred games. Twenty-six times I've been trusted to take the game-winning shot and missed. I've failed over and over again in my life and that's why I succeeded."

—MICHAEL JORDAN

Most of our lives we attempt to avoid failure. Somewhere we learned that failure is bad. Can you see that failure only shows up as bad if the context for life is trying to get somewhere or prove something? Shift the context to one of awakening, and it isn't much of a stretch to comprehend that failure is a vital part of the process. Most of us grow the most when faced with failure; it is a fertile ground for transformation. In the past I had been hiding in addiction, married to someone who drank every day, and in the failure of our marriage we both awoke to heal and claim our complete self. Not long ago, almost twenty years later, I received a note of forgiveness from my former husband which I saw as an acknowledgment of our journey together and a completion of that chapter of failure from our past.

We encourage our employees to fail, for if they are never failing they are playing it safe, which means they are living in a comfort zone and no longer stretching toward transformation. At Café Gratitude we celebrate our mistakes! If someone drops a glass, or forgets to enter an order into the computer, or delivers the wrong food to a table they call out, "I made a mistake!" This alerts the managers in case they need some assistance in cleaning the situation up, and it frees the person who made the mistake from getting stuck in humiliation, shame, or self-blame which would only further interfere with the service.

Matthew shared with me that when we opened our first Café Gratitude in the Mission District of San Francisco, he was free to play full-out, to entertain failure, because he wasn't attached to making it a success. Once he acknowledged that failure wouldn't mean anything other than the fact that the structure was insufficient to support and sustain what we were up to, then he could give it everything he had!

I, on the other hand, believe that failure happens every day, and it supports me in shifting my focus, directs my research, creates my to-do and to-be list. Failures tell me where something is needed or when something needs redirecting. It is my job to oversee and learn from failure. Failure is my ally!

From the beginning of our business we have served vegan ice cream. We started with small ice cream makers, and customers cranked their own. When we could no longer keep enough ice cream makers sufficiently frozen to supply the demand, we switched to a soft-serve machine. I tweaked an ice cream recipe for months to come up with one that could be made by our machine without freezing too hard or being overly sweet. This one was used for more than two and a half years, but it was labor-intensive. When I could no longer be personally present in the café tending to the constant needs of the soft-serve machine, our managers would complain about its many breakdowns. As we expanded and more machines were in place, the issue became overwhelming.

In response to this failure/opportunity, we opened ourselves to a new solution. We went into the ice cream business! We purchased a batch freezer and sold off our soft-serve machines. Now we make delicious ice cream in our central kitchen and distribute it to all the cafés in bulk containers. Our own product line with our proprietary labels on the products allows us to sell pints of our ice cream as well as Big Love bars (chocolate-covered ice cream bars) and I Am's (an almond cookie-ice cream sandwich). The "failure" of the soft-serve machines and my recipe led to our latest development, our own line of live, vegan, organic ice cream. "Failure" moved us in the direction of success—a much more exciting, delicious, and profitable product line that is supporting our company's expansion.

PRACTICE

Select a time in your life that you view as a failure, or evoke a particular event in which you believe you failed. Share with another person what that time or event was and why you consider it a failure. Now look and see what the lesson was, what you were being shown or taught. What did that failure lead to, what was the value of that failure, what did you learn? Can you now see how that failure contributed to your life, your growth, your business?

Switch and let your partner share with you. If you are not doing this practice with a partner, write it down.

19

Being Complete

We say that getting and staying complete is essential to being present. Consider that wherever you are incomplete, it interferes with your ability to be here now. We get distracted, fearful, and hesitant. Getting complete means being in communication, taking responsibility, cleaning the past up, so there is nothing between you and anyone else except love. Obviously this is ongoing; you don't get complete and then be done with it. Start taking on being complete at the end of each day. Look back over your day and see if you left anyone with anything that would create separation between you and them. Another way of looking at this is asking yourself, "How can I restore love to this person or situation? What do I need to say or what request can I make?"

PRACTICE

On a sheet of paper draw two columns. On one side write the name of anyone in your life where love isn't as present as it once was. In the other column opposite their name write one or two words that represent what is in the way—for example, anger, past debt, timidity. Continue until you can't think of anyone else. Do not overlook anyone. If someone's name comes up in your mind, write it down. Next to each name write a date by which you promise to get this complete. Don't give yourself too much time. This completion process could be a letter, a phone call, or a personal communication. Remember: taking responsibility, apologizing, and cleaning up the past accesses the power for being fully present now. Keep this practice in place, adding new names to your list as they surface.

20

The Freedom of Apologizing

We say leaders always take 100% responsibility and apologize first. It's not the truth that you, as leader, are always 100% responsible; it's simply a powerful place to come from. Consider that being 100% responsible extends even to how something you might have said was actually heard. When one person takes responsibility it is much easier for someone else to do so. If you are defending your viewpoint or hanging on to your cherished opinion, then very likely so too will the other person. Apologizing is the practice of giving up being right. We have shared the observation that human beings are nearly addicted to being right. Apologizing is a powerful antidote. What are you more committed to—being kind and empowering, or being right and domineering? Consider which approach your people will respond to best.

Recently someone posted their experience at one of our cafés on an online blog. She apparently had run into our café just after being mugged to use the telephone. Her report of her experience was certainly not favorable for the café, and she shared her opinion freely. I chose to write her, apologize for the experience she had, and promised to check into it. She posted my subsequent response clarifying the situation, which I ultimately did not feel we had mishandled, although I certainly saw how we could have been more hospitable. The blog continued, with many people adding comments calling my apology "damage control." Rather than being frustrated, I saw this as an opportunity to really share with others who clearly were not our usual customers who we are and what we are committed to. My apology was sincere, as was my taking responsibility for how the person was left. A few days later she clarified her report to more accurately represent the events of her experience and thanked me for writing. My apology had created an opportunity for us to connect and be in one another's reality.

PRACTICE

Share with a partner the name of someone you are making wrong, a person you have been unwilling to extend an apology to. What is your experience of him or her? What does your judgment rob you of? Now, practice apologizing to your partner as if they are the person you are making wrong. Be generous, take 100% responsibility. Afterward, note your experience and how it makes you feel. Now consider apologizing to that person directly.

21

Forgiveness Is a Gift

We define forgiveness as "to give as before," with nothing in between you and another but love. Forgiveness provides us with the opportunity to be completely present, no past in the space, and the freedom to freely give. When I received a forgiveness letter from my ex-husband, he wrote so beautifully that although he forgave me, he couldn't promise to forget, for human beings are fickle, but he would not dwell on the remembrance.

Whom can you forgive? With whom can you practice letting go of an upset?

If you are the recipient of an apology, practice returning to the level of nothing in between you and the person apologizing; no separation. What you can't forgive possesses you. Forgiveness is a gift creating space for your life to shine through to the maximum.

> "I, even I, am he who blots out your transgressions,
> for my own sake, and remembers your sins no more."
>
> —ISAIAH 43:25

PRACTICE

With whom are you still holding on to some hurt, some upset, some disappointment? What is unavailable to you as a result of this? What would it take for you to forgive him or her? Take that on.

22

The Culture of Human Resources

We relate to our human resource managers as the keepers of the culture. They are a resource for our people, staying shored up with our mission, being sure we offer—and they receive—the tools and education we promise. They hold the big picture and are there to support everyone in participating in the discovery and recreation of the experience of Café Gratitude day to day. Our experience starts with our people. If employees and managers aren't having a sacred experience, we won't be providing one for our customers.

For us a sacred experience is living the Oneness, being willing to get anything that creates separation out of the way. No wonder we say Café Gratitude is our big foolish project, like Noah's. Imagine creating a business that employs more than two hundred people and serves fifteen hundred customers a day, saying, "We are going to experiment in all being one."

What we call "sourcing humans" is maintaining the Oneness, listening for and having our employees learn to be responsible for any expressions of separation, without making them wrong for expressing it. Striking that balance is a bit trickier than you might think. Somehow, when people are in their separation they also start being very right about it; after all, there is always a lot of "evidence" to justify being a victim, being a martyr, being righteous, being separate. Evidence is what we create when we are being right. Who would you have to be to say, "I am creating being so justified in my feeling underpaid and overworked [separation] right now?" Imagine being that responsible for your own experience. Can you see the power in this question as well as the way out?

Our human resource managers stay tuned to the growth of our vision through our people and policies. The policies we envision and administer are designed to actualize our mission and maintain it, so that our people and our community (company) will thrive.

So many of our employees have taken risks in their own lives toward recovery from addiction, healing of parental relationships, health issues, past debts, intimate relationships, and much more. They know we will support and encourage them, be here for them, as they lean into the discomforts of their lives. Our employees often finance another employee's dream by pooling their money, knowing that the same will be done for them.

The culture of our company is one of unconditional love, and in that space the possibilities are endless.

PRACTICE

If you were creating the culture of your company (community), what qualities or characteristics would you list as most important? How would you see yourself fulfilling those qualities? Make a list of those qualities and briefly describe how you would fulfill on them.

23

Leaving People in Great Shape While Letting Them Go

We are proud of the fact that some of our employees move up through the company and some move through it. They take the training and education they receive and go out in the world to create their dreams. Perhaps they return to school, get married and start a family, pursue the arts, found their own business, or travel the world. We are here to support our people in dissolving whatever is obstructing their aspiration for living their dreams. If that dream includes Café Gratitude, that's wonderful. And if it doesn't, that's great too. If you choose to leave our company, we celebrate your choice. We believe that each and every employee has contributed something toward our vision, and we appreciate them for it. We consider that we have profited if our employee has grown, transformed, and is empowered. What Matthew and I are most excited about is our people. If we question ourselves or our commitment, we reinvigorate our inspiration by looking at our people and acknowledging their personal growth. Being a midwife and witness to the enfolding of that process within them leaves us nourished and fulfilled.

We are committed to the transformation of our employees' lives. They are students. We have created a system for reviewing their progress so they know what there is for them to be working on. If something isn't going well, we want to intervene and support them in having a breakthrough. We passionately desire and celebrate their success. The only time we would ask an employee to move out of our employment would be if they simply weren't up for the game we're playing. Otherwise, we don't give up on them, even if they are struggling.

When employees become aware of the magnitude of our love and concern for them as people they reciprocate, and this reciprocation profoundly enriches our enterprise at every level. We are eager to continually be creating them as who-we-know-them-to-be, which is, to put it succinctly, expressions of the divine. Sometimes that is not what all people are up for, however. People can be enamored with their limitations, and there is nothing wrong with that; it is just not what we are committed to, for you or for us. If we stop listening and creating our employees as their highest self, then we stop being our highest self, and then everyone's integrity is compromised.

One insight that has guided us to support our people's choices is the importance of being committed to them but not attached. If we start to relate to someone like we can't get by without them, we are placing unfair pressure on them to stay with us, consciously or unconsciously. We know that a partnership will always show up as win-win. We need not worry about someone leaving, for we are fully confident that another will step in, or step up, to stand on that person's shoulders and lead from where they left off. We empower an employee who intends to leave the company with the inspiration to train someone else to provide all and more of what they have contributed. In this way, the employee experiences being free to go, fulfilled and aware of their accomplishments before actually leaving. We celebrate one person's graduation—we cannot hold on to our "seniors" forever—even as we welcome the new person who takes their place.

On the rare occasion that we ask someone to leave, we let them know that they can always apply for a job with us again. It's up to them to get complete with whatever might be creating separation. If we aren't complete with them, it is our responsibility to communicate and complete whatever that might be. In some extraordinary eventuality in which we would choose not to rehire the person, we let him or her know why we are making that choice, so there is no mystery or secrecy concerning their possible future with us. If it clearly isn't a fit, then we support them on whatever path they are in pursuit of. We are for our people.

24

Work as Play/This Is It

We are living in a culture that boasts TGIF (Thank God It's Friday). Mostly we survive work so we can get to play, or we are so addicted to work that we don't know how to relax and play. In other words, we are always trying to get somewhere else, and we are left with the experience of "this isn't it," and some other life must be more fulfilling. It is better over there than it is over here. Doubting what we are doing with our lives is one of ego's main ways of keeping us separate from love, our true state of being.

One night before closing, after a long day at work I realized that we were always trying to get home if we were at the café, or get to the café if we were home. It was crazy-making. When I could just be "this is where we are now," my experience was completely different: when we are home we are home, when we are at the café we are at the café. My entire body relaxed.

If you aren't loving what you are doing, why are you doing it? No matter where you are, be there; fall in love with where you are, it's magical. Have your work be a practice in choosing. When at work, choose it—that's freedom.

25

Creating Games

There are a lot of ways you can look at your goals. We choose to relate to our aspirations as games. All games have guidelines; otherwise it would be difficult to play and keep score so that you know where you are and what you have to play for. Games have a beginning and an end. Games present opportunities to become complete and re-commit. They are inspiring. You see the possibility in them, and they are fun. You and your people enjoy playing them.

At Café Gratitude we play daily, monthly, quarterly, and annual games. Managers often create games for shifts to play: can the servers get someone at every table to laugh? Can a server offer such a delectable invitation for sweets that every table orders a dessert? There are endless possibilities for playing the café game. Games offer a delightful impetus and constant opportunity for our employees to stretch, inspire, and enthuse. The games we play with our management team cause them to keep looking at their responsibilities from a variety of perspectives: what is happening in their cafés; who are our top servers; how quickly our food and beverages are being served; the extent to which our customers are acknowledging their servers through tips; how many new customers we are seeing each day; is there anything else our customers wish we were providing?

Any feedback or outcome you are striving for can be created as a game. Games keep everyone united on the court rather than isolated in the stands—two very different experiences. It is one thing to be playing a game; it is another to be watching it.

One of our four key insights is "be in the game." There are many games we play at Café Gratitude. You can create games that fit your company/community profile and culture. Here are more of the games we love to play.

THE ONE GAME

We know that if we hung signs in front of our cafés that announced "The Last Supper served here tonight," our entrance would be jammed with people trying to get in, and the line would extend around the corner, no matter what their religious beliefs. The grandest game is to provide such a sacred experience for our customers that they can't help but be talking about it to everyone they meet. No matter what else happened in their day, their meal and experience at Café Gratitude lives foremost in their hearts and minds that day. Imagine experiencing being so in the presence of unconditional love that you knew yourself as love; love moved through you and was you, a passionate lover of unspeakable and everlasting beauty of mind, body, and spirit! Any feelings of separation disappear; love is all there is. Ultimately, that is the victory in the game we are playing.

What would it take to experience no separation? Who would we have to be for ourselves and others? We are always fortifying ourselves for this visionary challenge: what is the gap between what we offer and what we say is our mission? What can we be responsible for, and what do we see that would make a difference?

We couldn't possibly provide the experience of unconditional love if our people weren't present to how great their lives are. This is the game that all of our employees enlist in. Can you keep your attention and your worship power on how great your life is now, no matter the circumstances you may be dealing with?

We say try this on, like an experiment, and see what shows up. We are done with the old game of trying to get what we want, strategizing, and trying to feed the hungry ghost that never provides satisfaction or fulfillment. We know that what we experience is what we have our attention on, so let's put our attention on Wholeness and Oneness, on the qualities of the divine to which we aspire. All our other games are created to support these two: 1) our provision of an unconditional love experience, and 2) the realization of how great our lives already are.

Ushering in a new paradigm, a world of Oneness, requires that we let go of what we already know, of what "makes sense" to us. How else are we going to create a sharing society? Perhaps that is the most foolish of our projects, to go first toward sharing, without concern for who might not be willing to play.

BREAKTHROUGHS

Breakthrough binders are found in every café. In these binders our employees write out what breakthrough they are currently experiencing; in what area of their life they would love to have some new freedom, some new possibility made manifest. They express it in their own handwriting and place it in the binder, and our managers are responsible for reading and reviewing it and supporting and coaching employees in the direction of having that breakthrough. The breakthrough could be in any area of their lives. When one of our employees has achieved a breakthrough in a particular area, they aspire to a new breakthrough and write about that one in the binder. In this way our people are always working in some area of their life that matters to them each day they are at work, and we are supporting them in living an unimaginable life.

"In the beginning was the Word,
and the Word was with God,
and the Word was God."
—JOHN 1:1

AFFIRMATIONS

One of the fastest and most efficacious means for creating a new life is to get the process rolling verbally. The same old things we have been saying to ourselves and to others are creating the life we already have. That doesn't mean your life isn't great, but if you aren't experiencing how great your life is, start affirming in spoken words what it is you want or desire your life to be. We say, give away what you want to experience! The interesting thing about verbal affirmations is that some people think they don't work. Yet when you look at what you are already affirming (and we are always affirming something), you can see that it is what you already have or already are. Notice also that your internal dialogue never doubts the power of those negativisms which you verbally affirm that tend to diminish yourself. Often when we overhear a friend or relative say "I'm a loser" or "I'm no good," we intuitively intervene and counsel them by responding, "You are diminishing someone I love."

We seem to instinctively know that verbalizing negativisms keeps our loved ones—and by inference, ourselves—small, weak, insignificant, and lost. But we tend to overlook the positive corollary: that verbalizing our own goodness and victorious greatness also has power. Often we deny this, however, and become argumentative about it. Cynics have said, "Affirmations don't work."

However the multi-billion-dollar advertising industry knows they work. Look at their fabulously lucrative advertisements. Advertisers know what cynics don't: that repeating the same affirmation over and over again works. You, their audience, retain it and can easily recall it. One of the most powerful tools we have access to is our self-talk—saying to ourselves aloud what we would love to be hearing.

Speak to yourself as you would speak to someone you cherish dearly and esteem highly. Listen to yourself speaking, as your words are expressing the divine. Words have power to heal and power to destroy. "In the beginning was the word." Start to access the universal circuitry by affirming the best that you can be, by placing your attention on it now.

We have placed the power of this "divine best" that's at the heart of the universe at the center of how we order and serve food at Café Gratitude. Every item on our menu is a high and holy affirmation. It's part of what makes our cafés so attractive to our customers. They find themselves playing a game they didn't expect in a restaurant setting, and consequently being thrilled by its uniqueness at the same time that they are partaking in an exchange of sacred commerce.

GENERATING

We don't often relate to the thoughts we are having as if we are the ones generating them. It just seems like those are the thoughts we are having. Consider that we actually generate our thoughts, and you could generate any thought. It is a practice. The thoughts you generate are the ones you have practiced. Practice thinking and sharing the highest and best thoughts about yourself and others.

QUESTION OF THE DAY

Every day a question is asked of every customer; that is how the game is played. The question begins at the head of the company each morning and is passed along throughout the company as part of the daily clearing. The questions are always about eliciting some sort of opening to our customers, some new way of viewing or acknowledging some area of their lives. So many miracles have arisen from this question of the day, even with people who resist it. We received an e-mail from a man who was in our café on a day when we asked, "If money were no consideration, what would your life be for?" He wrote us that for years he had been suffering through a job he hadn't enjoyed, and as a result of our question and the gracious listening of his server as he responded with his answer, he found the resolve to quit his old job and start the new career he had always dreamed about. He was thanking us for encouraging him to finally take the leap and make that change. He shared how happy and free he felt.

We had a female customer who intensely disliked being asked the question of the day and always responded "no" when asked if she would like to hear it. We didn't give up on her, but rather continued to ask her whenever she came to eat if she would like to hear the question. One day the woman arrived with her son, and as it happened, we forgot to ask her about the question of the day. She and her son then took on creating what they might ask if they were the ones inventing the question that day! Our son, Ryland, who is one of our managers, went to her table to check on how she was doing, and she shared with him her appreciation for coming over to her and always asking if she wanted to hear the question of the day. She said that her son had just given her one of the most meaningful gifts of her life through what he had shared in answering the question of the day which they had both created. As you can see, in spite of her outward irritation, this woman had looked forward to our expression of interest in her and her thoughts by our putting the daily question to her. When it was not asked by our people, she created the opportunity it provides for herself and her son.

Our question of the day has become something we are renowned for and something people visit our cafés to be asked. People are looking for ways to have more meaningful conversations, and they just need a little encouragement to engage. Our daily question is something we provide that exceeds our customer's expectations. No matter what business you are in, there are always customers, clients, vendors, or investors you could be asking questions of that would inspire greatness.

WELCOME

We are committed to having each and every customer welcomed into our cafés just as our guests would be when they come into our homes. We invite our employees to be bolder and braver than ever before in ensuring that everyone is welcomed as they come through our doors, especially if it is going to be a moment or two before we can attend to them. We also invite our servers to guide our customers through our menu, making sure they know all that is available, taking on really hosting them through their experience.

GIVING SOMETHING AWAY

When we opened our first café we had an alarm clock that we would set to ring randomly a couple of times a day. When the alarm went off, the next person who ordered was given the item for free. This game was intended to keep us in the flow, to remind us that giving something away is a way to ante up, stay in the game, raise the stakes. Remember: releasing into the flow is the same as receiving; giving and receiving are one and the same.

I MADE A MISTAKE

By celebrating mistakes we create what we call a "shame-free zone."
So often are mistakes the cause of our feeling ashamed that we
even lie and attempt to cover up mistakes for fear of being shamed.
In our business we play a game of calling out loud, "I made a mistake" whenever someone has lapsed in the quality of their service.
We overheard a table of businessmen commenting at lunch that
they would love to have that practice in their office; how liberat-
ing that would be, how real and safe they would feel.

NO GOSSIP

We have a no-gossip policy. This is a noteworthy game we play.
Nothing will destroy the integrity of a company faster than gossip. We distinguish gossip as anything that is said or listened to
that diminishes a person in someone's hearing. In other words,
gossip is often something you probably wouldn't say if you were
saying it directly to the subject of the gossip. We say, if you have
a committed complaint, then be sure you are talking to someone
who can do something about it, beginning first with the person
with whom you have the issue.

LAUGHING OUT LOUD

Children have a great deal of freedom to laugh for no apparent
reason. We on the other hand pay to go to a comedy club and then
sit and question whether the comedian was humorous or not. Exer-
cising the latitude and creating the space for adults to laugh out
loud without a specific reason is a health issue: laughing boosts
your immune system, releases endorphins and serotonins, expels
toxins, and relaxes muscles. There are laughing clubs in India as
well as laughing yoga. We create a game of laughing out loud to

interrupt any recurrent thought of limitation that one might be experiencing. In our cafés you can often hear someone start laughing and others spontaneously joining. This practice could be incorporated into any environment.

HOW IS YOUR LIFE?

Imagine having a manager take on being responsible for your life being great and checking in with you from time to time to see how you're doing. At Café Gratitude, we play that game. It's so much more interesting to take on being a contribution to others' lives than to always be concerned for your own. We'll have employees take on making sure another employee's shift is great; their job is to look out for them and to cause their shift to be extraordinary. Not only will you strengthen your team but you will raise the bar for what is possible at work. Your people will start looking for ways they can contribute to one another rather than just doing their own job.

NO COMPLAINING FOR TWENTY-ONE DAYS

When someone first mentioned this game to me, I was inspired. It didn't sound difficult, until I attempted it. I couldn't believe how often I complained, and I would never have said I was a complainer. Our household took it on together, and it was so much fun. Matthew decided after a couple of days that the rest of us should keep going and he would take on complaining for all of us! I was surprised by how much opened up for me when I stopped complaining. So many opportunities started presenting themselves while I was practicing saying, "Wow, that's great," no matter what came at me. Talk about priming the pump for the non-ceasing flow of everything! I highly recommend this game. Remember, this is twenty-one consecutive days of no complaining whatsoever, so if you complain even a little, you simply start over at day one. Good luck and be ready for a flood of possibility.

COMMUNITY SEATING

At Café Gratitude we share tables, so there will often be two couples who do not know each other sitting together, or a couple of single people at a table with another party. This is one way that we practice sharing. We say that sharing a table is practice for sharing the Earth! Although some people request and wait for a table that doesn't require them to share, we always encourage it. In the first three years of business, there were three marriages (that we know of) between people who had met at Café Gratitude while sharing a table. In fact, our first-ever wedding cake was made for one of these marriages.

At one of our all-employee meetings an employee shared that a man has been coming into the café to be in our environment while he works to complete a film he is writing. Another man had been seated at the same table and the writer had argued with himself in his head as to whether he was going to speak and acknowledge the other person or just keep working quietly. He chose to interact, and before the other man left he handed the writer a check for $25,000 to put toward the completion of his film.

Our game environment has inspired employees to create and enroll other employees in games in which they see possibility residing. Recently, several employees took on not going shopping for one month. They did a clothes swap, made meals from scratch together, cleaned out each other's apartments and rooms. We have employees not drinking alcohol for a month, or seeing how many new friends they can meet in a month. Games are not "just for kids." Actually, empowering loving games are a great way to keep your environment exalted and empowered. We do play games that make a difference!

SALES

Sales are our way to invite our customers to have an enriched experience, to increase their awareness of what we offer. If we only take their orders, we are not providing them with the full service we are committed to offering. We want our servers to let our customers know what we offer in terms of ingredients, preparation, and how those appeal to the customer's personal desires and expectations, as well as to their spirit of adventure and discovery. In this way customers can knowledgeably choose what they would like. We encourage our managers to know where their cafés are, in terms of sales and the relationship among sales-totals, "break-evens," and profitability.

We celebrate every dollar earned as a sacred exchange. We are committed to creating a sustainable company that supports the lives and families of all our employees. Our managers create daily sales games that inspire them and their teams, along with games like tip percentage, superfoods added to smoothies, time lapse between seating and greeting, and any consideration that would enhance our customers' experience. People don't want to be sold, but they do want to be enlightened so they can make informed purchases. We are more aware than ever that we vote every day with the dollars we spend. People want to vote wisely. They want to be part of the solution.

ACKNOWLEDGMENT

There are so many ways we could take on appreciating and recognizing our customers. We could thank them for choosing a vegan meal today, or for bringing a friend with them, or for answering the question of the day. Every day there are endless opportunities for us to appreciate and acknowledge. Start creating an environment of appreciation at your office or company.

WHAT ARE YOU GRATEFUL FOR?

Shifting your attention to what you have to be grateful for will always intervene in some experience of scarcity and get you present to all that you already have and fulfillment as an inner quality. It isn't possible to be given more until we appreciate what we already have. And remember to include yourself on the list of what you are grateful for!

26

The Inevitability of Oneness

"Free will does not mean that
you can establish the curriculum.
It means you can elect
what to take at a given time."

—*A COURSE IN MIRACLES*

We all have this lesson of Oneness. We can choose how much we will resist, how much we'll suffer. Consider that the universe, the one song, is always working together for the awakening of all. Divine Mind cares only for wisdom and doesn't distinguish between life and death, rich and poor, right and wrong, good and bad; it knows no opposites only degrees of consciousness, degrees of Oneness. We get to either partner with the melody, consciously join the song, or sleep through choir practice and indulge in aloneness and separation until it is just too painful.

Really look at your life. What is the condition of your body, your finances, your relationships telling you? What are you resisting? Look at your world, the wars, the blame, the bickering, the self-ishness, the arrogance, the intolerance. What is the message of this melody? Notice the quality of the air, the water, the soil, the oceans, the forests, the quality of the lives of those who have and those who have not. Don't make anything wrong, just listen: what is the hymn calling forth? What is missing that its presence would make a difference?

We suggest that all signs lead toward dissolving into love, attending to the whole, gifting your life. We are hearing the chorus say, "Put your individual wants and deficiencies aside; your petty little problems aren't worthy of your majesty. Surrender your comforts and attend to your whole body—this lifeboat Earth and the well-being of all its crew. These other distractions fall short of your grandeur."

> "For whoever will save his life shall lose it;
> but whoever shall lose his life for my sake,
> the same shall save it."
> —MARK 8:35

What might this creation look like for you? For us it may be company-sponsored community housing, the sharing of automobiles, co-raising of our children, second-hand clothes on healthy bodies, shifting away from the paradigm of looking good to the sustainability of all our choices. A bold end of accepted cultural expressions of separation.

If you've read this far, we want to acknowledge the reader for considering making your life about the whole community, for looking at holding the seat of Oneness in a business environment. It is heroic to even consider standing before the cynicism and resignation of contemporary culture and lighting a candle for communion in the workplace. The demons of survival and scarcity, fortified with an arsenal of quarterly reports and stockholder fears, will attempt to swallow you. As I write this, we are preparing an investment plan to raise money for Café Gratitude's expansion. I am confronted by how our proposal, particularly how our return on investment and the company valuation, will be received. There are moments when my egoic doubting mechanism anticipates rejection from the "real" world, the real players. But mostly I keep faith and see that investing in Café Gratitude is about letting go of compiling money to buffer ourselves from a scary dysfunctional world. That's the old program. *"How's that working?"* Café Gratitude is about creating a heart-based culture against the social tide of the exalted, insatiable "me." Our investment partners are those moved by themselves and by a daunting dream, and they are courageous enough to risk their resources for this big foolish project. Why would I want any other kind of partner?

The couch is now a fence; what was comfortable **is** no longer. Regardless of what is calling you, we invite you to find your way to serve the Oneness, to make your life about the whole of life and know yourself as God.

> *The sage accumulates nothing,*
> *but the more he does for others*
> *the greater his existence;*
> *the more he gives to others,*
> *the greater his abundance.*
>
> —LAO TZU

27

Sacred Commerce Isms . . .

- Lean into the discomfort.
- Nothing is personal, they are not responding to you.
- Safe is a sedative.
- All there is is love; everything else is our resistance to it.
- Emotional adversity is just like the weather, let it move through.
- There is nothing wrong.
- You don't have complaints, complaints have you.
- What would love do now?
- What you resist persists.
- Suffering is a call for awakening.
- Everything can be resolved through communication.
- What would it take to restore love now?
- Are you more committed to being right or to workability?
- Look at what you have an abundance of now; that is what you are worshipping.
- There are no others.
- It's all you.
- It's all made up.

- Whatever experience you are having, you are the one creating it.

- The present moment is inevitable.

- If you are not failing often, you are playing too small a game.

- It's impossible to acknowledge someone too much.

- Just let go of your opinions and everything will be clear.

- Choose what is.

- Everything is teaching you something.

- Knowing keeps you from experiencing.

- Everything is working on your behalf.

- There is nowhere to get, nothing to prove.

Recommended Resources

BOOKS

The Abounding River (board game) by Matthew and Terces
Engelhart

The Abounding River Personal Logbook by Matthew and Terces
Engelhart

The Diamond Cutter by Geshe Michael Roach

Focus on the Good Stuff by Mike Robbins

Peak by Chip Conley

Plenty of Time by Terces Engelhart

The Soul of Money by Lynne Twist

WEBSITES

www.cafegratitude.com
www.landmarkeducation.com
www.pachamamaalliance.org
www.stayhuman.org
www.circleoflifefoundation.org

About the Authors

Matthew Engelhart's business ventures always aspire to shake up the existing paradigm. He grew his Flax Clothing line, an all-COD company—unheard of in the garment industry—that was run out of an old dairy barn in central New York, from one treadle sewing machine to a $28-million-dollar-per-year business. Currently he and his wife and business partner Terces are the owners of Café Gratitude, a popular organic vegan restaurant chain with more than two hundred employees and four locations in the San Francisco Bay Area. The cafés, which support local farmers, sustainable agriculture, and environmentally friendly products, serve living, organic food made with the freshest ingredients possible. In 2007, Terces Engelhart published *I Am Grateful*, a recipe and lifestyle book based on the restaurant.

Together, the Engelharts published *The Abounding River Personal Logbook* as well as The Abounding River board game, both of which focus on their practice of being in abundance. In addition, they facilitate workshops on abundance as a quality of the Divine, the Kindred Spirit-spiritual relationship, and Sacred Commerce, merging the sacred with the commercial. Terces also facilitates One Week Without Sugar, an introduction to a spiritual diet. Some of their workshops are combined with yoga and living foods on their organic farm in Maui. The Engelharts, who have been featured on radio and television, live in community with two of their five children in San Francisco.

Notes

Notes